A Christian Perspective
of Postmodern Existentialism

A Christian Perspective
of Postmodern Existentialism

The New Humanism of Western Culture

John D. Carter

RESOURCE *Publications* · Eugene, Oregon

A CHRISTIAN PERSPECTIVE OF POSTMODERN EXISTENTIALISM
The New Humanism of Western Culture

Resource Publications
An Imprint of Wipf and Stock Publishers
199 W. 8th Ave., Suite 3
Eugene, OR 97401

www.wipfandstock.com

PAPERBACK ISBN: 978-1-7252-9263-5
HARDCOVER ISBN: 978-1-7252-9264-2
EBOOK ISBN: 978-1-7252-9265-9

06/04/21

Unless otherwise noted all Scripture is taken from the New American Standard Bible (NASB)

THIS WORK IS DEDICATED to my many Carter relatives*, both living and deceased (in no particular order): Alvin Pleasant**, Norris***, Janice Ruth, Mazella Jane, Ronald Fay, Brett Jonathan, John Quillen, Nancy Colleen, Emily Elisabeth, Donald Ray, Hadessah Lynn, Judy Arleen, Robert William Jr., Sylvia Marie, Jack Quillen, Maddax Dean, Walter Maynard, Daniel Ray, Georgia Francis, Chad Daniel, Franklin Gregory, Ida Ethyl, Louis D, George Franklin, Horton Lucian, Phoebe Nadine, Cori Cherrise, Billy Ray, Kelly Odell, Marilyn Jane, Janie Belle, Maxine Frances, Jocelyn Ann, Amelia Yvonne, Wanda Carol, Naomi Nicole, Shawn David, Ryan Joseph, Bobby Gene, Angela Kay, Brooke Angela, Larry Kelly, Sheri Gwynne, Allie Gertrude, Kelly Marie, Luke Daniel, Ava Elliana, Isabella Jane, Robert William, Richard Kelly, and Anna Lee.

*With exception of the first two names, only those bearing the Carter name, whom I currently and personally know, or those who I have personally known, are included in this listing.

**my fourth cousin of the famous "Carter Family" (the first bluegrass recording artists) who passed when I was 11 years of age.

***My great-great-great-great grandfather who was an early pioneer in the mountains of Virginia. He was born in 1748 when Virginia was still a colony of Great Britain. His hand-built log cabin, in whose interior my son and I have freely roamed, is extant and on display at Natural Tunnel State Park, Scott Co., VA

I know, Lord, that a person's way is not in himself,
Nor is it in a person who walks to direct his steps.
Correct me, Lord, but with justice;
Not with Your anger, or You will bring me to nothing.

JERIMIAH, PROPHET OF YAHWEH, SEVENTH CENTURY, BC

God is not merely good, but goodness;
goodness is not merely divine, but God.

—C. S. LEWIS

Contents

Author Note

I THINK IT PROPER here to give the reader a forewarning of my writing style. While my writing here deals with many complex issues in philosophy, theology, science, sociology, history, etc.—all of which I put into a strong Christian framework—I have tried to write in a more informal style than one might normally find in such a volume. The reader might be surprised when he or she finds that I occasionally allude to a favorite pastime of mine, namely, my interest in various aspects of motorsport, and even other anomalies which might not seem, to some, to fit into the spirit of the subject at hand. I hope these occasional informal excursions will not offend my reader, because I think that this approach can soften the blow of what might be perceived by some readers as uncomfortable subject matter. Some of the statements and conclusions I make in this book will be unsettling to some readers, but that is not my intent. I am just an ordinary Christian, albeit with some education, who has a strong interest in not only the things of God, philosophy, and science, but also in many other matters as well. While I can sit in my favorite chair reading books on philosophy, theology, and science for extended periods of time, I can equally enjoy many hours with either my Martin dreadnaught or my steel guitar, playing my favorite Hank Williams songs. Therefore, I do not try to disguise the less serious side of my personality as I write on the very sobering, and eternally important, subject matter of this volume.

Preface

THIS VOLUME IS A sequel to my earlier 2005 book, entitled: *Western Humanism—A Christian Perspective: A Guide for Understanding Moral Decline in Western Culture*. Although secular scholarship often associates the term Humanism with a positive worldview,[1] it is clear both from the title of my prior book as well as the present one that I do not present Humanism in a positive light. Of course, there are some aspects of Humanism that must be considered in the light of moral advancement. Any genuine Christian would certainly be wrong if he were to frown upon the humanistic endeavor of President Abraham Lincoln to free the American slaves from their dreadful bondage. No doubt, Lincoln's initiative was based upon Christian convictions, even though some historians have questioned the depth of Lincoln's understanding of, and commitment to, the Christian faith. Nonetheless Lincoln's motivation was, without doubt, consistent with the principles of justice taught throughout Scripture.

The unfortunate prevailing belief among contemporary humanists is that the concept of morality, i.e., the knowledge for standards of right vs. wrong, can be separated from the God of Holy Scripture. However, the whole concept of morality must be found in the creator of all that is, namely Jesus, the Christ. There can be no absolute standard for morality outside of God's will for humanity as it is revealed in Scripture.[2]

Since my prior book defended a worldview based upon the authoritative precepts of Scripture against a humanistic worldview (where the

1. Throughout this work, I use the term "worldview" to mean the viewpoint that one holds regarding their concept of ultimate reality and, thus, the term is not necessarily confined to a "world" that implies the earth or even that of the entire universe.

2. It is imperative that the reader understand how I am using the word "morality" to fully comprehend the meaning of this paragraph. I expound upon that meaning in the *Introduction* which follows.

authority of Scripture is either denied or little regarded), that book was, therefore, intended for those who acknowledge Scripture as the supreme guide for living a genuinely good and purposeful life. When I first began authoring that book, I was comfortably employed as a professional scientist at a Fortune 500 industrial research laboratory, a position I took after having received the PhD in polymer science from one of the leading schools in that field. Polymer science—also known as macromolecular science—is the science that deals with the chemistry, physics, and engineering of plastic and rubber-like materials. Even the well-known biological macromolecules that are integral to the functioning of all living organisms can be classified as naturally occurring polymers. Deoxyribonucleic acid (DNA) is probably the most readily recognized bio-polymer by the public. The impetus for writing that first book was to fulfill what I regarded as a higher purpose than what was then my employment as an industrial scientist. As such, my goal was certainly not financial gain which sometimes comes from writing.

However, with the constraints of leading a family, building and setting-up a new home, and staying up-to-date in my professional field, the progress of writing that first book was cumbersomely slow. In fact, so slow that had it not been for an unforeseen turn of events in my scientific career, that book may have never come to completion. That unforeseen event was the result of a severe downturn in the business of the corporation for which I was engaged in research. Since I was involved in fundamental research, the type of research which often yields little immediate effect on the bottom line in corporate America, I was considered expendable. Therefore I, and many of my colleagues, lost our research positions. This event was more unfortunate for the corporation than it was for me, because unbeknownst to research management, I was at the point of discovering what I had been laboring for many years to accomplish. My discovery would have made a definite payoff in the company's technical advancement, but that involuntary incentive into early retirement created for me an opportunity that I welcomed. I remained quite positive about the situation because I knew that I would be able to concentrate on finishing the book that was languishing in the wings simply because of a lack of time. The goal of completing that book, I knew, had more significance in the overall scheme of my existence than did the goal of succeeding at industrial scientific research.[3]

3. I returned to the industrial scientific community shortly after completing, publishing, and promoting my first book before permanently retiring from my work in the chemical and physical sciences.

Up to the point of my departure from scientific research, I had not given much thought to how I would proceed with publishing the book, but with new found time on my hands I decided that I wanted to accept the challenge of self-publishing. With that decision made, upon completion of the manuscript, I did not send it to any publishing company, but at once immersed myself in gaining a working knowledge of the publishing business. The decision to self-publish came about primarily because of my desire to have the experience of doing it. I have always been interested in learning and knowing how anything in life works.[4] However, there is no doubt that my decision to self-publish the book had an impact on the book's obscurity. Additionally, I did not seek out any endorsements by well-known scholars in the field of philosophy, religion, or history to splash on the dust jacket as is the usual custom in book publishing. Usually the positive review-bits found on book jackets have been specifically solicited for the sole purpose of gaining book sales, and I am sure that many such informational tidbits have been displayed simply for either the sake of friendship or the return of some type of owed favor. I would even suspect that many such blurbs have been printed without the commentator having read even more than a few pages (or no complete pages at all) of the work on which they are commenting. It was for these reasons that I did not seek out noted commentators to "advertise" on the jacket of that prior book. It was the scarcity of feedback from the Christian community that made me question the wisdom of writing a follow-up book on the subject. However, I became especially aware of the need for further work on the subject since, in that book, I did not deal with Postmodernism. One reviewer lamented that I had not discussed the impact of Kierkegaard on Western thought, and the more I thought about that complaint the more I realized the criticism was justified.

But I think that there must be nothing more encouraging to any author than reading a review of his or her work where genuine appreciation is expressed by a random reader. Many years after the release of that book, I came across an obscure review that gave me new impetus to write the

4. For example, I find it hard to understand how those who use the automobile every day of their lives, and yet have absolutely no understanding of how it works, are content with themselves. That quest for understanding, no doubt, is what inspired me to completely remove and disassemble the motor of one of my automobiles, and after reassembly with new internal parts, use it carefree for more than an additional 100,000 miles. I did that unusual feat for the purpose of gaining additional knowledge of modern computer-controlled internal combustion engines, and thoroughly enjoyed the journey. My appreciation and enthusiasm for the old-car hobby continues to this day. The decision to self-publish was driven by that same spirit of adventure.

follow-up book that is now the subject of this preface. While traveling to Southeast Asia I went online to the Google Books website from which my prior book was at one time available. I was expecting to be greeted there with the familiar message that I had seen so many times before: "This book has not yet been reviewed." But unbeknownst to me at that time, the United States and other countries are often serviced by separate servers, so content that might appear in one part of the world, may not be seen in other portions of the world. To my surprise there was a review from a far-away reader in India that was very gratifying to this author and supplied one of those confirming moments that my effort in writing was a worthwhile one. In commenting on my first book the reviewer wrote:

> I am basically a trainer in psychology. I have read many books to keep myself updated with the views and opinions of great thinkers. This book demolished all the theories that I thought were a threshold to success. In fact, I am now planning to design another training program to encourage people not to depend so much upon the self-help gurus. This is the best book I have read in my life. When I read a book, I usually underline those lines that appear important to me. There are books where I would have underlined 10 lines maximum. That's the most I think worthy in those books. Here I have literally underlined every page. Great effort. Keep it up. I would like to personally meet the author. Dr. Abraham P Ruby, Bangalore, India[5]

Thank you, Dr. Ruby, for those kind words of encouragement. Maybe someday we can indeed meet. With that encouragement, I have taken the step to write this second book on the subject of Western Humanism. Although this book stands alone, the reader will benefit from having knowledge of my prior book, and so I would encourage the reader to become familiar with that book. Both books are written in the same vein, i.e., both books consider the term Humanism in a negative context. By that I mean that I define the humanist as one who seeks his ultimate value, his ultimate

5. Ruby, "Google Book Review." This review eventually appeared on the domestic Google server, but unfortunately it was later removed. Likewise, a previous positive review from a *Library Journal* reviewer was taken down when the book was first published many years prior. Furthermore, *Google* at one time had the authorship of this book assigned to a different John Carter than myself, and after I contacted them, they corrected that error, but then at some time later that same error reappeared. I get the impression that maybe *Google* wishes to suppress the content of this book, as it definitely goes against the world spirit of Humanism to which they strongly adhere. (I have edited this review for spelling and grammar since the author's first language is apparently not English.)

purpose, and his ultimate meaning in human-being, in lieu of finding those ultimate values in the Ultimate Reality of all reality, i.e., the being of the God of Scripture, the true and only source for reaching those goals.

I stressed in my prior book that it is a gross error to assume that Humanism is synonymous with atheism. While the humanists who identify with the term "secular humanist" are usually indeed atheistic, many other humanists will accept the existence of deity. And, of course, there are some who call themselves "Christian" who seem to revel in identifying themselves with the label of Humanism. However, these "Christians" will often hold to positions that are incompatible with the God revealed in Holy Scripture. For example, if one calls himself or herself a Christian humanist and then does not acknowledge the destructive influences of the seriously sinful practices currently running rampant in Western cultures, I identify that Christian as a "Non-Secular humanist" with little essential philosophical distinction between him or her and atheistic humanists. However, in those rare cases where genuine believers try to reclaim the term "Humanism" and use that term to make it compatible with Scripture, I would emphatically urge those persons to carefully define what they mean whenever they wish to identify positively with that term. Given the fact that the word has been totally hijacked to become synonymous with either total rejection of the fundamental doctrines of the Christian faith or disingenuous Christian belief, it makes me wonder why any genuine believer would want to identify as a humanist. The situation is similar to the term "fundamentalist." Even though I can identify with that term, in the sense that there are certain fundamental Christian beliefs that are necessary for genuine Christian faith, the term no longer means what it used to mean, mainly because of media distortion, and I can therefore understand why one would want to shy away from identifying with it. Furthermore, it needs to be understood that many people are humanists in this negative sense without calling themselves by that title. So, no matter where one stands in the spectrum that spans from atheistic Humanism to a Humanism that acknowledges the existence of a supreme being, it is my hope that this work might help the reader reconsider the thought processes that have made his or her philosophy of life to be one that is yet wanting the truth that all people, consciously or unconsciously, are seeking. With the meaning to which I attribute to the term Humanism clarified, let us now begin our consideration of Postmodern Western Humanism.

Acknowledgements

I AM PARTICULARLY INDEBTED to my friend Sarah Stallings Hale for her expertise in the English language. Her many suggestions significantly improved the effectiveness of my writing for which I am exceedingly grateful.

Introduction

BEFORE WE BEGIN THE subject of Postmodern Humanism, I must first define what I mean by certain terms involved in the subject. The meanings of both terms, Postmodern and Humanism, can be confusing since they can differ depending on the one using them. I use the terms Secular Humanism, Non-Secular Humanism, Modern era, and Postmodern era often throughout this work and the reader needs to know how I am using them for a proper understanding of my writing.[1] Although I touched on my use of the term Humanism in the *Preface*, I think it here useful to further develop that definition. As in my prior book, I am using the word Humanism to describe a system of thought where one falsely believes that he or she has sovereignty over his or her own moral nature. To use the words from the *Preface* of my prior book, Humanism is a system of thought which teaches:

> . . . that man, in the power of his own nature, can function as a moral being, but it is a system where that capability does not truly exist. Humanists hold to a system of a perceived morality, but [humanistic philosophy] leads away from true morality[2] because they [humanists] do not understand that true moral knowledge is only reached when Scripture is recognized as a supernatural revelation of God's mind to humanity. To believe that man can be truly moral—outside a genuine relationship to the God of Scripture—is a gross error in thinking.[3]

---

1. Because I am using these terms in a specific sense, I use capitalization to indicate that specificity wherever they appear in this volume.

2. My use of the phrase "true morality" here equates with the term that Scripture uses—righteousness—to indicate the same thought. A word study of that term, from a biblical perspective, should clarify this concept.

3. Carter, *Western Humanism*, i. (I have here slightly modified some of the wording for clarification.)

Furthermore, I distinguish Secular Humanism from Non-Secular Humanism by simply using the criterion of belief in any deity. For example, I regard the ancient Greek Presocratic philosopher Xenophanes as a Non-Secular humanist because his beliefs had a theological element, even though those theological beliefs were pantheistic. On the other hand, I refer to the Sophist Protagoras as a Secular humanist in that he, as well as his fellow Sophists, did not regard anything as real that could not be perceived by the senses. In other words, I refer to those who do not acknowledge the existence of deity—be it the God of Scripture or some other—as Secular humanists. (See Figure 1 for a timeline linking Secular and Non-Secular Humanism with Western history.[4]) For the purpose of this work, I will say that the Modern era began near the beginning, or towards the middle, of the nineteenth century and that the transition from the Modern era to the Postmodern era occurred at about the midpoint of the twentieth century, the time acknowledged by many historians of philosophy as when existentialistic worldviews began to dominate in Western culture. Therefore, the Modern era identifies with the beginning and the maturing of the Industrial Revolution, which came on the heels of the Western Enlightenment. At the beginning of the twentieth century, the burgeoning Industrial Revolution had not reached its full potential, and its proponents were focused on creating the massive assembly lines of heavy production that came to represent the era. But more importantly, Einstein was at the doorstep of formulating the mathematics of both general and special relativity, and the mathematical formulation of quantum theory was also in its initial stages. The scientific progress that followed the development of modern physics was revolutionary, as it provided for a new understanding of the structural fundamentals of physical reality.

Unfortunately, in my preceding book, I did not identify the transition from the Modern era to the Postmodern era. In that book I traced the historical development of Modern Western Humanism beginning with concepts found in ancient Greek philosophy and going forward to those found in the Enlightenment. The Enlightenment led to the unprecedented success of the scientific method in the late nineteenth and the early twentieth century, and this resulted in the growth of the Secular humanistic worldview. I characterized Secular Humanism in Modern Western culture as primarily influenced by the writings of Charles Darwin, Frederick Nietzsche, Sigmund Freud,

---

4. Page xxv. Obviously, this chart is nowhere near exhaustive, but it should help the reader put my writing into a proper time perspective.

and Karl Marx, while ignoring the significant Postmodern philosophical developments of the mid-twentieth century. In so doing, I made the mistake of identifying much of the moral failure which we are seeing today in Western culture solely with Modern Humanism, even though much of that failure is better identified with Postmodern Humanism.

This oversight should not be too surprising given the state of our current educational environment, both in our Western secular and Christian educational systems. Many of our leading contemporary Christian scholars have failed to make the distinction between the Postmodern and Modern eras. Francis Schaeffer, the well-known Christian philosopher/apologist/theologian of the latter part of the twentieth century, who was influential in my thinking, wrote on both Modern and Postmodern Humanism making no real distinction between the two. For example, although his brief book *Escape from Reason* is in large part concerned with Postmodernism and less concerned with the Modern Humanism stemming from the Enlightenment, the term "Postmodern" appears nowhere in the text.

Surprisingly, the lack of acknowledgment of any influence of Postmodernism continues to persist among some of our best contemporary Christian minds. I once listened to a Christian radio program where the question of the relevancy of Postmodern influence on current worldviews was being addressed.[5] The context of that discussion was centered on a debate between Dr. William Lane Craig and Dr. Myron Penner. Professor Craig is becoming increasingly well-known as an excellent and formidable Christian apologist, and Penner is an Anglican priest who had recently published the book entitled, *The End of Apologetics: Christian Witness in a Postmodern Context.* In that book Penner posited the idea that apologetics based in the rational methods of the Enlightenment is a serious existential threat to genuine contemporary Christian faith. At the beginning of their discussion, in defending the validity of an apologetic witness, Craig made the surprising declaration that the idea of Western culture being now in a Postmodern context is nothing more than a myth, "perpetrated in our churches by misguided youth pastors." That Craig could make such a misinformed statement is indicative of just how Postmodern influence has crept in unexpectedly. But the fact that Penner is arguing from an existentialistic position makes Craig's declaration a paradoxical one. Obviously, Craig is correct in defending the need for apologetics, for even Scripture commands it. In Scripture we read of the injunction to "always be ready to

---

5. Craig vs Penner, *Up for Debate* hosted by Julie Roys, Moody Radio, April 2016.

make a defense to everyone who asks you to give an account for the hope that is in you, yet with gentleness and reverence."[6] Of course, that command will be relevant as long as time exists. But the fact that Penner is himself a postmodern who is arguing from a Postmodern position means that Craig cannot effectively engage him. If Craig will not acknowledge the Postmodernism from which Penner is addressing the issue of apologetics, then there is little that can be said to convince Penner of his error. To bolster his argument in this exchange, Craig made the point that the books written by the likes of Dawkins, Harris, and Hitchens[7] would have fallen flat if indeed the atheistic Modern position was losing its relevancy.[8] But there are two clear misconceptions in this statement by Craig, the most obvious being the assumption that the atheistic position equates with a Modern position. As in Modern Humanism, there is both a Secular Postmodern Humanism (i.e., an atheistic Existentialism as seen in the philosophy of Sartre) as well as a Non-Secular Postmodern Humanism (i.e., a religious Humanism as in the Existentialism of Jaspers.) Secondly, while the atheistic authors that Craig referred to want you to believe that their arguments are based on the rules of pure logic and, therefore, give the illusion of working in a Modern mode, I hope to show here that the spirit of atheistic Postmodern Existentialism is functioning behind the scenes, where the rules of logic are put aside in deference to a willed outcome.

In his classic work on Christian apologetics, *An Introduction to Christian Apologetics*, John Edward Carnell, writing when Existentialism was first gaining its foothold in American culture, began by rightfully framing his book's introduction in a Postmodern existentialistic setting in lieu of the classic defense of Christianity against the Modern scientific worldview Craig sees as his primary mission. Of course, as an academician, Craig's approach to Christian apologetics is a useful one because atheistic Modern Humanism is yet alive and thriving in academia. But Craig needs to acknowledge the need for a Postmodern approach to the same subject because of the Existentialism that now commands the thinking of the majority in Western culture.

6. 1 Pet 3:15.

7. Example books by these authors to whom Craig here refers are Richard Dawkins's, *The God Delusion*, Bantam, Sam Harris's, *The End of Faith: Religion, Terror and the Future of Reason*, W.W. Norton, and Christopher Hitchens's, *God is Not Great*, Hachette.

8. I will show in chapters 2 and 8 that Dawkins, although claiming scientific rationality, is in reality operating more in the vein of Existentialism.

But sometimes even when Christian academic scholarship acknowledges the reality of the distinction of the Modern worldview against that of the Postmodern worldview, the understanding associated with that distinction can want clarification. For example, in his book *Above all Earthy Pow'rs: Christ in a Postmodern World*, Professor David Wells of Gordon-Conwell Seminary commented upon the failure of the Enlightenment ideal which has opened the door for the Postmodern worldview. Wells separates Enlightenment Humanism from the process of modernization in Western Culture. He writes:

> What gave this Enlightenment ideology its staying power and plausibility, I have suggested, was that fact that it came to prominence as the Western world was being reshaped and transformed by modernization. It is because of modernization, and not really because of the Enlightenment, that the West has moved from being premodern to being modern in its organization . . . Had modernization never happened one wonders if the Enlightenment ideology would have sustained itself for very long. As it was, however, the Enlightenment thinking came to dominate how the West has thought about life. Today, however, the growing complexity of the social fabric is probably what has contributed to the crisis in which the Enlightenment world finds itself. Enlightenment ideology is being taken down. As so often happens at junctures like this, we are hearing in the collapsing Enlightenment world the "swan song of a dying epoch . . . ."[9]

Notwithstanding the admiration that I have for Professor Wells work, I must respectfully disagree with his analysis at this critical point. Certainly, Enlightenment ideology is being taken down, but the Enlightenment ideal and the explosion of knowledge that resulted from the extraordinary successes of the scientific method cannot be separated from the onset of modernization and the Industrial Revolution. The Enlightenment, science, and modernization are all intimately linked, and they all have an important bearing on each other. It is my contention that the breakdown of Enlightenment ideology began, and continues its progress, because science has ventured into philosophical arenas where it has no authority and, by so doing, it has seriously damaged its own authority. The only authority of science comes from the scientific method, i.e., knowledge which is authoritatively gained from repeatable experimentation in the laboratory. But unfortunately, science is now making absolute declarations where the experimental

9. Wells, *Earthly Pow'rs*, 31.

evidence for those proclamations simply does not exist. I will deal more extensively with these concepts as the book unfolds.

Hopefully, this book will help the reader understand the primary issues that have led to a demise of the Enlightenment ideal in Western culture, and to an understanding of the issues that have brought on the onset of the existentialistic worldview. In chapter 1—Part I (Historical)—we will first review the basic philosophical principles that make up the movement known as Existentialism. Then in chapter 2 I introduce a few aspects of the transition that took Western culture from the materialistic atheism that is identified with the Secular Humanism of Modern thinking to the Existentialism that has become prevalent in contemporary Western culture. Here I use the work of Professor Robert Flint of the University of Edinburgh who brilliantly wrote on the materialistic atheism of the nineteenth century, when the Humanism of the Modern era was establishing its foothold in Western civilization, which would eventually transition into the Humanism of the Postmodern era. In chapters 3, 4, and 5, we will look at the lives and work of three influential Western Existentialists. In Part II (Contemporary) we will look in greater detail at the mechanisms, with specific examples, that have led to the contemporary existentialistic worldview that now dominates Western culture. Finally, in the last chapter, I emphasize why existentialistic Humanism should be of great concern for the Christian. Just as the Modern Humanism that grew out of the Enlightenment had a devastating effect on the Christian church, existentialistic Humanism is likewise taking its own negative toll on that same church today. The tragedy is, of course, that it seems to be happening without our awareness. It is my hope that this book will bring light to that metamorphosis.

Figure 1 Western Humanism Timeline

Key: Light Grey-approximate time of activity: Dark Grey-insignificant activity

Time Line	Secular	*Example Philosopher(s)*	Non- Secular	*Example Philosopher(s)*
			Presocratic	Thales, Xenophanes
500 BC				
	Sophists	Protagoras		
			Classical Greek Philosophy	Plato Aristotle
Birth of Christ				
			Early Church	Pelagius
500 AD				
1000 AD				
			Scholasticism	Aquinas
1500 AD			**Renaissance**	Erasmus
	Enlightenment	Hume	**Enlightenment**	Kant
	Modern	Nietzsche, Marx	**Modern**	Kierkegaard
2000 AD	**Postmodern**	Sartre	**Postmodern**	Jaspers

PART I

Historical

1

What is Existentialism?

MY INTRODUCTION TO EXISTENTIALISM came by way of Wesley Barnes's introductory book entitled *The Philosophy and Literature of Existentialism*. I purchased the volume at the US Army post exchange while serving as a young soldier in Fulda, Germany. During that time, I was a thoroughly lost young man, and I was reading various authors trying to understand the turmoil of the times. Western culture was then undergoing an unprecedented upheaval because of various issues involving socialism, communism, racial injustice and what many people, particularly those of my generation, believed to be an unjustified American involvement in Vietnam. That war was still in progress, although it had by then begun to wind down from its peak.[1] Professor Barnes's book was one of the *Barron's Education Series* publications, and it was a good introductory work to the subject of Existentialism. My own thoughts were being pulled in an existentialistic direction, away from the Christianity of my childhood, and I was struggling to reconcile those early Christian influences with the facts of life that I was then observing daily. Upon the careful examination of Barnes's book, I began to understand Existentialism and its implications in the social unrest of that era. Barnes stated in the preface to his primer, "Our contemporary films, plays and newspapers carry the movement [Existentialism] and are carried by the thesis of the existing

---

1. While my advanced infantry training was in Vietnamese-style jungle warfare, it was President Richard Nixon's decision in 1971 to begin the pull-back of American involvement in Vietnam that was responsible for diverting my deployment from Vietnam to Western Germany.

individual who strives for identity and meaning solely in and through his own terms."[2] It is important to note that the common thread of any humanistic worldview (be it Modern Humanism, the subject of my prior book, or Postmodern Humanism, the subject of the present book) is man's quest for meaning and purpose "through his own terms," i.e., through human terms.

The Dane Søren Kierkegaard, a professed Christian,[3] turned the philosophic focus away from society to that of the individual. He was the first to interpret phenomenal reality within the relativity of each existing individual. Thus, in Existentialism, the significance of existence becomes primarily what any given existing individual interprets it to be. In Existentialism, all reality is relative to the individual who perceives, simply because of his existence, and this essentially translates into morality becoming relative to individual conscience. Therefore, Kierkegaard bears great responsibility for the contemporary idea of the relativity of ultimate truth. It is in Existentialism that the concept of "what is true for you is truth for you, but what is true for me is truth to me" becomes a falsely perceived reality.

Therefore, in Existentialism, the concept of absolute truth goes out the window, and reason becomes jeopardized as it becomes suppressed in existentialistic thinking. Although the goal of existential Humanism is consistent with the goal of Enlightenment Humanism, the former Humanism strives for that goal primarily through human volition while the latter Humanism strives for that goal through the guidance of reason. Both forms of Humanism strive for meaning and purpose through human terms, whether or not the existence of God is acknowledged. Furthermore, the rise of evangelical Christianity in Western culture, with its emphasis on individual salvation through one's own choice, has possibly contributed to the onset of an existential religious Humanism that seems to be in competition with an understanding (i.e., an understanding which is consistent with Scripture) of the truth of Christianity. Existentialistic thought, in general then, is characterized by the suppression of the rational aspect of human personality in favor of an acclaim to the sovereignty of the volitional aspect. Some practical and easy-to-understand examples of this principle in action should be instructive to the reader, as they will show firsthand how existentialistic thinking has led to false concepts of reality in our Postmodern culture.

2. Barnes, *Existentialism*, v.

3. Actually, Kierkegaard often claimed that he was not a Christian, a questionable ploy he used to emphasize that no one could, in reality, achieve Christ's perfection.

Some Practical Illustrations of Existentialism in Postmodern Western Culture

Recall how many times you have heard parents and educators tell their young subjects something like, "You can become anything you want to be if you are willing to work hard enough." But this often-quoted maxim is simply not true. I was recently watching a national news program which featured for their closing story a segment that told of a blind high school football player who had scored a touchdown on a goal-line-stand in a regulation contest. When interviewed the young blind student stated proudly that his goal was to play in the NFL. Of course, such courage and drive can be admired, but realistically any person who understands the game of football knows that young man is striving towards an unrealistic goal. Some responsible person in that young man's life should help him direct his noteworthy drive towards a goal that is more reasonable. Many blind people have made admirable contributions to society but certainly not as NFL running backs. The existentialistic idea that the exercise of one's choice can accomplish anything that he or she might desire is certainly perpetuating a false reality.

As another practical example from my own life experiences, I once attempted to tutor a student who was taking a course in college algebra with the goal of being admitted to nursing school. No matter what method I used in my attempt to help that student understand the concepts of algebra, there was simply nothing that worked. No matter the amount of effort the student exerted, the intellectual capacity to understand the essential elements of algebra was simply not present. The false idea that one can achieve a goal simply from the desire to do so is a result of the Postmodern philosophy of Existentialism. While an existentialistic society may find a way to award an individual with an IQ of 100 an MD degree, I certainly would hope that if I were to be admitted to an emergency room—clinging to my life because an errant driver had turned into the path of my antique R69S, a machine that has inferior stopping power compared to that of contemporary motorcycles—that ER would not be staffed by a group of like physicians and nurses! Of course, I am saying this with tongue-in-cheek, but nonetheless there is a genuine reality mirrored in that sentiment.

A final practical contemporary example is given from the world of American politics that demonstrates the acquiescence of reason for the sake of placating an irrational demand that was made by an existential observation. Earlier in her political career, the thoroughly humanistic Hillary Clinton made a statement that came back to haunt her when she was seeking the Democratic party's presidential nomination in 2016. In 1996, when campaigning for her husband Bill Clinton's presidential re-election, she attempted to defend her husband's 1994 crime bill. That bill was introduced to allow for the use of enhanced policing to control the increasing violence of gang related criminal activity occurring in America's most populated cities. In so doing she made the statement:

> We need to take these people on. They are often connected to big drug cartels. They are not just gangs of kids anymore. They are often the kinds of kids that are called 'super predators,' then-first lady Hillary Clinton said, according to a C-SPAN video. "No conscience, no empathy. [sic] We can talk about why they ended up that way, but first we have to bring them to heel.[4]

This rhetoric, while not particularly egregious, was simply a strong way of saying that society needs to be diligent at enforcing the law to get control of the crime problem in question. The inducement and enforcement of law is, of course, a most effective tool that the humanist has at her disposal to affect control of human behavior. But because of the preponderance of existentialistic thinking in Western culture, Ms. Clinton was forced to back away from her original statement, even though it was based in a rational and factual position. The implementation of President Clinton's enhanced policing policy resulted in an increase in the arrests of black Americans. When that enhanced policing policy resulted in occasional incidents of excessive use of police force against the criminal element, black Americans began the movement called "Black Lives Matter" (BLM) to protest increasing incidents of police misconduct.

When Hillary Clinton was leading a fund-raiser to support her bid for the Democratic Presidential nominee in 2016, a protester, representing the "BLM" movement, rudely interrupted the proceedings, and requested that Ms. Clinton apologize for "mass incarceration." The protester stated, "I'm not a 'super predator,' Hillary Clinton." But Clinton, instead of addressing the situation in a rational manner by insisting that she had not called her (the protester) a super predator, was quick to acknowledge that she had originally misspoken. So here we see the situation of a skewed reality brought about by an existentialistic mindset. Ms. Clinton was not guilty of calling the "BLM" protester a super predator as the protester was

4. Scott, "Black Lives Matter Protesters," para. 6.

implying. But instead of pointing out that reality to the protester and standing her ground, Clinton gave way to the protester's irrational position most likely because it was the path to the least resistance for maintaining peace in that situation, and causing minimal damage to her political goal. The importance of keeping peace in that problematic situation, brought on by the irrational position of the protestor, outweighed the need to address the situation in a rational manner.

Of course, Existentialism is obviously more involved than acknowledging this acquiescence of truth in order to achieve a willed outcome. While this defining acquiescence is certainly characteristic of the philosophy of Existentialism in general, it represents only the most basic of concepts that are observed in the main ideas that make up the existentialistic worldview. Before we go forward to examine the thought processes of some of the major philosophers responsible for both the introduction and maturing of existentialistic thinking, we will investigate some of the main ideas that better define what is meant by Existentialism. The term has an inherent abstraction that makes defining the subject challenging.

The Convenience of Existentialism

In considering why the Existentialistic worldview is becoming so prevalent in Western culture, to even include the culture of Western Christianity, it is necessary to acknowledge that its adaptation to contemporary reality is often because it provides a pathway that offers the least amount of resistance to a consciousness that wants to be at peace, at all cost, with itself and its surroundings. The development of existentialistic thought in Western culture can be likened to the flowing of water down a mountainside. Flowing water always takes the path of least resistance, and so it is with the development of Humanism which has matured with the appearance of Postmodern Existentialism. The existentialist sees what exists and stops there, developing his or her perceptions of reality by observation of what appears to exist, without any consideration of why it appears as it does. An intellectual insight that wants to probe *why* what exists, does exist, is suppressed in Existentialism, often for the sake of convenience as was pointed out in the above example with Ms. Clinton's response to the BLM protester. For the existentialist, the most important aspect in any consideration of reality is the existence of what exists, and not the reason it exists.

To help the reader better understand what I am driving at let us consider a couple of examples that the Christian reader will be able to identify with. We read in Scripture repeatedly that Jesus is the *only* way to eternal life. Jesus stated, "I am the way the truth and the life, no man cometh unto the Father except by me," and again, "And there is salvation in no one else; for there is no other name under heaven that has been given among mankind by which we must be saved," and one more, "He that believeth on the Son hath everlasting life: and he that believeth not the Son shall not see life; but the wrath of God abideth on him."[5] Of course, I could go on with many more examples which explicitly declare this point, but these should suffice to get the idea across. Now the point that I am trying to make is that this observation will no doubt trigger in many minds, the question: Would God condemn the person in a faraway land who has never heard the name of Jesus? The person with an existentialistic bent will probably reason that there exist many people who have never heard the name of Jesus, and therefore, he or she might conclude that here must surely be an example where an exception to the claims of Scripture is warranted. For the sake of keeping the reader's interest alive, I will stop here with this example and pick up on its exposition in chapter 6 after I more fully develop the error involved in Postmodern existentialistic thought. Another example follows:

The late Vincent Bugliosi was the California prosecutor who prosecuted Charles Manson and wrote the bestsellers, *Helter Skelter* and *Outrage*. He also wrote *Divinity of Doubt: The God Question*. In *Divinity of Doubt* Bugliosi presented his case for his agnosticism and insisted that the Christian God could not exist because God (i.e., the Christian God) would necessarily be inconsistent with the scripturally derived attributes of God.[6] Specifically, Bugliosi made the point that because of the incessant suffering and injustice witnessed in the world on a daily basis, the Christian God, if he existed, could not be both omnipotent and morally good.[7] According to Bugliosi a morally perfect God would not allow evil if it were in his power to do so. And of course, this is a question that is always addressed in philosophical debates regarding the existence of God. In my earlier book

5. John 14:6, Acts 4:12, John 3:36 (KJV).

6. One of the first subjects of study in Christian theology consists of understanding the attributes of God. There the student of theology learns that God is Omniscient (all knowing), Omnipresent (everywhere present), Omnipotent (all powerful), Immutable (unchanging), morally perfect and just, meaning that he is holy, righteous, benevolent, and merciful.

7. Bugliosi, *Divinity of Doubt*, 25–37.

I discussed C. S. Lewis's book *The Problem of Pain* which dealt extensively with this subject. So here is another example of an apparent existing reality, which appeared to Bugliosi as an injustice, and from which he drew his philosophical conclusion of agnosticism. Is Bugliosi's existential observation and subsequent conclusion a valid one, or has his Existentialism led him to deadly error? Again, for the sake of keeping the reader's interest alive we will pick up the discussion later in this chapter after we more fully develop a proper biblical view of human nature.

Existentialism, Scripture, and Human Nature

Because Existentialism is, without doubt, a Postmodern Humanism, it must be defined within a concept of human nature. A humanistic philosophy always implies a position on what constitutes human nature, and this is true of Existentialism. It is one's conception of human nature that ultimately determines one's philosophy of living. The classical Greek philosophers taught that human nature was bent towards the moral good and that the intellectual nature of man could enable one to understand the nature of that good. Subsequently, the will could then be directed to move an individual towards that ultimate good. Socrates believed, erroneously, that through a rational understanding of the nature of good, virtue could be taught and subsequently learned. The teaching of virtue would thereby activate the will to achieve that good.[8] In all forms of Humanism, human volition is believed to be sovereign, or free, to act. In classical Greek Humanism, the will follows the intellect to the good that it finds through the process of reason. Therefore, in the Humanism that is derived from classical Greek philosophy, the essence of man is viewed to be such that man has the potential to achieve virtue—or moral wholeness—if the intellect is taught to function properly.

The principle of defining a philosophical position from a concept of human nature even applies to a biblically based Christian philosophy, which we sometimes refer to as a "Christian worldview." In both Hebrew and Greek Scripture, the concept of human nature revolves around the reference to the "heart" of man. When Scripture refers to the "heart" of man, it is not referring to the blood pumping organ which every human being possesses. While that physical organ is central to the physiology of the body, the "heart," of which the Bible usually speaks, is central to the

8. Carter, *Western Humanism*, 6–9.

9

intangible personality of human existence, by which every human being's nature is characterized. While the heart, or personality, varies uniquely with every individual, there are nonetheless universal traits which characterize the "heart" or the nature, of every human being. For example, we read in the prophet Jeremiah's writing that "The heart is more deceitful than all else and is desperately sick; Who can understand it?"[9] Thus, we know from Scripture that the human heart, in its natural condition, has a bent to dishonesty and moral wrong. Empirical observation, both internal and external, should give to anyone who might desire it, evidence of the reliability of that declaration. Thus, the Scripture's characterization of the human heart provides for us an understanding of human nature that is based in reality or, in other words, based in truth. Concepts of human nature that go contrary to scriptural teaching are always in error, and thus, the humanistic understanding of human nature is usually in opposition to scriptural precepts.

The concept of the "heart" as it relates to personality is not only important for understanding human nature but is also important in understanding the nature of God. We learn that God is a person by the fact that Scripture refers to him as having a heart. God is a person, meaning he thinks, he feels, he acts and, therefore, exercises volition. We read in Scripture that when God "saw that the wickedness of man was great on the earth, and that every intent of the thoughts of his heart was only evil continually," he "was sorry that He had made man on the earth, and He was grieved in His heart."[10] So, we here observe that God experiences the emotion of grief. His heart was troubled as he reflected on what human nature had become because of Adam's disobedience. Furthermore, it is clear from Scripture that God clearly has an emotional nature. Indeed, the Scripture tells us that God is love; thus, his personality is even described primarily in emotional terms.[11] I remember a teacher from one of my childhood Sunday School classes who defined "the heart" as the "seat of the emotions." For some reason that definition has remained with me even to this day. And while I now believe that definition is oversimplified, I can understand how one might conceive of such a definition. Certainly, a primary quality of personality is in its emotional nature. When we refer to a person as being narcissistic, anxious, or even psychotic, we are assigning to that person a

9. Jer 7:19.

10. Gen 6:5–6.

11. 1 John 4:8.

characteristic that is emotional in nature. But the important idea behind the biblical concept of the heart, both the heart of God and the human heart, is the fact that it makes existence as having an essence that can be characterized by attributes that describe the nature of that being's existence. In the introduction of my earlier book, I reminded my reader that even the atheistic Freud acknowledged that the basic nature of man was characterized by what he referred to as the id, the part of personality that best corresponds to the emotional aspect of human nature.

Throughout Western history, there have been differing opinions as to what are the dominating attributes of human personality. The primary characteristics which define the essence of man have been debated since formal philosophy originated with the ancient Greeks. But the one thing that was acknowledged, until the onset of Existentialism, is the fact that human nature has an essence, even if the nature of that essence might be debated. It is readily clear in both the era of the classical Greek philosophers and in the era of the Enlightenment, that the rational aspect of personality was acknowledged as the dominating attribute of human personality. Certainly, throughout history there has been a struggle between those who view rationalism and those who view Romanticism as being the primary characteristic that best describes the primacy of human nature. In Romanticism the emotional aspect of personality has sought to diminish the dominance of the rational.

However, unlike the Humanism that was birthed in Greek philosophy, human nature in existential humanistic thinking cannot be described outside of a given single individual. Every individual has a nature that can only be described in terms of the experiences of that given individual. In other words, there is no universal essence that can be used to describe human nature in general. As in the classical Humanism of Greek thought, Existentialism holds that every human being begins all experience with a blank slate and that his destiny, including his moral destiny, is *entirely* dependent on the choices that he makes. Modern Humanism holds that the intellect can enable moral living. But in Existentialism the classical struggle between the rational and emotional nature of man has no bearing on individual existence. The existentialist thus rejects any claim upon the nature of his existence that is derived from the historical struggle between these two dominating attributes of human nature. In other words, the existentialist admits to nothing that can describe him—all there is, is existence. This contrasts with the traditional claims that man has an essence that is inherent to human nature. The Modern humanist maintains that the intellect can decipher the moral good, and from that understanding human volition will induce the heart to follow the intellect, which in-turn will result in moral wholeness. In existential Humanism, human choice unconsciously acts to placate one's emotional nature with no deference to the rational essence of human nature, and thus the act of putting reason on the shelf serves to put truth into a relative light.

And of course, this makes Existentialism incongruent with Christianity. Absolutely central to Christianity is the fact that because of Adam's disobedience, all humanity has inherited a nature that is at enmity with God, and central to that fallen nature is man's separation from his Creator. In other words, the essence of man is morally corrupted because of Adam's disobedience. As a result, all humankind is damned because of an inherited nature that has a propensity to sin or, to say it differently, has a propensity to moral wrong or a propensity to do evil. That inherited fallen nature has affected man's entire personality, i.e., his emotional, volitional, and intellectual faculties. With the fall of man, human volition became impotent of its own accord, to choose entirely of its own accord, the moral good. Thus, the essence of man is morally corrupt, and of course this is the source of the prophet Jeremiah's description of the human heart that was mentioned previously.

And this brings us back to the example discussed at the beginning of the chapter where Bugliosi attempted to defend his agnosticism. Those who deduce from the problem of pain that the Christian God cannot exist, as did Bugliosi, are in gross error because they fail to understand the magnitude of the unfathomable abyss that exists between fallen human nature and the absolutely perfect nature of God. At the root of that misunderstanding is their failure to recognize the utter despair of human nature when it remains separated from God, and that failure ultimately leads to the blindness of their own condemnation. As the Scripture makes so plain "He that believeth on him is not condemned: but he that believeth not is *condemned already.*"[12] When one comes to the supernatural knowledge of the natural condemnation that all people are under when they remain separated from God's grace, he or she will then understand how even the air that one breathes is undeserved. God owes no one anything but damnation, because of human rebellion against him. Therefore, it should be clear that the essence of God is separate and distinct from the essence of his human creation. This is an important truth that is often overlooked by Non-Secular

12. John 3:17, (KJV, emphasis mine).

humanistic philosophers such as the late Dr. Wayne Dyer. As noted in my prior book, Dr. Dyer wrongly taught that the essence of man and the essence of God were identical, and this serious error has led many to believe in unscriptural, (i.e., false) concepts of God.[13] While human beings were created in the *image* of God, the *essence* of God is clearly distinct and far removed from that of his human creatures.

In Barnes's defining of Existentialism, we see that human volition has displaced the prominence of the emotional and intellectual aspects of human nature which are observed in Romanticism and classical Greek philosophy, respectively. Barnes writes, "The existentialist has for his religion his consciousness of experiencing. This continuous but varied consciousness of existing becomes a deification of his feeling and sensing through choosing, willing, [and] deciding . . . ."[14] In other words, his personality becomes defined through his ability to choose and decide. The existentialist has become responsible for his own being, solely because of his perceived freedom to independently choose. Barnes is here showing the precedence that the volitional aspect of human personality takes over the rational aspect. For the existentialist, in the consciousness of experiencing, volition becomes the supreme aspect of personality. The existentialist perceives that he has total freedom to choose, and it is this perceived freedom to choose that defines his existence. Barnes goes on to write:

> His freedom [the existentialist's] must be saturated with the snarl-like emotions of agony, despair, disgust, and the feeling of being absurd. Such must be the case because he can never use the words "I have made the right decision." There are no standards against which he can equate that which is "right." Having declared all consciousness of a thing other than his existing self as non-certain and without purpose, he can never have any object "out there" in what we call the real world of people, ideas, and things. His freedom consists in "choosing."[15]

However, because the existentialist is not free not to choose, his existence also relegates him to an enslavement that produces despair, disgust, and the feeling of the absurd.

Before we go on to examine Existentialism in more depth, I think it would help to reiterate and emphasize that the most practical (but in a

13. Carter, *Western Humanism*, 215.
14. Barnes, *Existentialism*, 6.
15. Barnes, *Existentialism*, 10.

pejorative sense) outcome of the existentialistic worldview is that it sacrifices reason on the altar of human volition. Existentialism leaves its subject with the false impression that the exercise of individual choice, with nothing to guide that choice apart from the goal of minimizing inevitable despair, is the primary function of existence.

Existentialism and the Concept of Despair

This section will briefly illustrate on what is meant by the "snarl-like emotions of agony, despair, disgust, and the feeling of being absurd"[16] that Barnes identified with the existentialistic position. To help in this endeavor I will review the work of Olson because he was more thorough in the treatment of this aspect of the subject than was Barnes. The concept of despair in the subject of Existentialism is realized in ideas of existential anguish, and the consideration of this subject will demand delving into deeper philosophical concepts. If the reader wants to skip over this section, I am content to leave that reader with the impression that Postmodern Humanism is sufficiently characterized by the three primary characteristics of Western Existentialism. These are (1) the loss of the concept of absolute truth, (2) the exercise of volition at the expense of reason, and (3) the gross error that Existentialism does not recognize an essence that characterizes human nature.

A popular conception of the nature of existentialistic philosophy is that it is primarily nihilistic in character. This sometimes leads to the belief that nihilism is the source for the concept of despair which we are here considering. But such a conclusion, as Olson points out, is somewhat misleading.[17] As defined by Merriam Webster, nihilism is "the belief that traditional morals, ideas, beliefs, etc., have no worth or value" or "the belief that a society's political and social institutions are so bad that they should be destroyed." While the belief that Existentialism is nihilistic may have an element of truth, it would be wrong to say that the movement is so nihilistic that the existentialist sees no value in the pursuit of the emotional contentment which all people naturally desire. Kierkegaard, the champion of Christian Existentialism, and Sartre, the champion of Secular Existentialism, whose lives we will review in later chapters, both experienced substantial material wealth and personal fame. It is also probable that they both derived a certain amount of emotional contentment from their pursuit of a

16. Barnes, *Existentialism*, 10.

17. Olsen, *Intro to Existentialism*, 1–29.

philosophy which they perceived would lead to a better understanding of the human condition.

In my earlier book on Modern Western Humanism, I discussed the primary means through which the Modern humanist seeks his emotional contentment. The Modern humanist attempts to find his fulfillment, i.e., his meaning and purpose, through his pursuit of wealth, his pursuit of pleasure, and his pursuit of social acceptance. These values often serve as the primary goals which are perceived as paramount in what is more commonly known as the pursuit of happiness. While the existentialist might pursue these same goals, he nonetheless correctly perceives that pursuit will not yield the emotional contentment that the classical humanist usually expects those pursuits to yield. The result of that failure causes the acceptance of the despair that is found in Existentialism.

Most students and enthusiasts of philosophy can usually detect at least some element of truth in the writings of all of the noted philosophers of history. And in Existentialism there is no exception to this observation. One of the positive aspects of Existentialism is in the genuine understanding that there is indeed truly little *ultimate* emotional satisfaction that comes from the accomplishment of the usual goals that most people believe will bring them fulfillment. But the existentialist's error is in the fact that instead of turning to Christ because of the false promises of Enlightenment Humanism, they choose—in this inevitable dissatisfaction—a sort of satisfaction in the despair of their dissatisfaction.

Olson separated existential anguish into three parts: "the anguish of being," "the anguish of before the here and now," and the "anguish of freedom."[18] The "anguish of being" results from the contingency of being or, to use the words of the existentialist, the "absurdity" of being. As Olson tells us, the absurdity of being does not refer to being as being ridiculous, but it refers to the result of the realization that being, as contingent, means that non-existence or non-being is just as possible as is existence. It is this realization that creates what is called in Existentialism "the absurdity of being." It is in atheistic Existentialism that the "anguish of being" is especially poignant because, as Olsen tells his reader, "since God alone could conceivably give meaning to being and since he does not exist, being is totally meaningless."[19] Therefore, the existentialist, be he conscious or unconscious of his Existentialism, views the whole of reality as an absurdity.

18. Olsen, *Intro to Existentialism*, 30–63.
19. Olsen, *Intro to Existentialism*, 36.

Olson shares an excellent quote from William James that demonstrates first-hand the spirit of the "anguish of being" that is found in Existentialism:

> James states that it is precisely at the moment when a man feels he has explained all particular natural phenomena: "that the craving for further explanation, the ontological wonder sickness, arises in its extremist form. As Schopenhauer says, *'The uneasiness which keeps the never resting clock of metaphysics in motion is the consciousness that the nonexistence of this world is just as possible as its existence.'* The notion of nonentity may thus be called the parent of the philosophic craving in its subtlest and profoundest sense. Absolute existence is absolute mystery, for its relation with the nothing remains unmediated to our understanding."[20]

And quoting Ludwig Wittgenstein, Olson again demonstrated the connection between the concept of the "contingency of being" with anguish. "Not *how* the world is, is the mystical but that it is . . . We feel that even if *all possible* scientific questions be answered, the problems of life have still not been touched at all."[21] Thus, the reader should note the clash between the existential worldview with the purely scientific worldview that came about from the Enlightenment.

The idea of the "contingency of being" has long been used as an argument for the existence of God. Indeed, it was a major argument of Thomas Aquinas, and even today it is used by Professor William Lane Craig (the Christian apologist previously mentioned) to combat the Modern Secular Humanism that is yet prevalent in Western academia. Craig is known for illuminating the Kalem Cosmology argument, which goes as follows: (1) If the universe began to exist, then the universe has a cause of its beginning. (2) The universe began to exist. (3) Therefore, the universe has a cause of its beginning. Thus, religious Existentialism, in this case, is consistent with the Judeo-Christian teaching that the universe, of necessity, had a beginning, a truth that some Secular humanistic scientists in the Modern tradition are trying to disprove, particularly through the discipline of cosmology. However, the scientific hypothesis of the "big bang" (and its general acceptance as fact within the scientific community) has opened the door for a scientific realization that the universe began at a specific point in time. Because of the philosophical implications of the "big bang," however, it is not too surprising to find that the late atheistic cosmologist Steven Hawking, and many of his

20. Olsen, *Intro to Existentialism*, 33.
21. Olsen, *Intro to Existentialism*, 33.

atheistic colleagues, worked diligently (and continue to do so) to refute the necessity of a beginning point in time for material reality. It is as if the scientific evidence for the beginning of the universe jeopardizes their desire to remain atheists. It is interesting that scientists in the vein of Steven Hawking have exerted so much effort to remain rational in their atheistic positions.

However, as Olsen so correctly pointed out, the philosophical difference between atheistic and Christian Existentialism is rather minimal.[22] The only fact preventing the perception of "anguish of being" in anyone is to have the knowledge that one's sin will not be held against him or her because of the sacrifice of Jesus Christ. Unfortunately, in Christian Existentialism the idea of alienation between God and mankind because of human sin seems to be less important in the overall scheme of existence than is the alienation from man's fellow beings. As we have previously discussed, for the existentialist there is no defining human nature that characterizes human-being (in general), and it is this conclusion that flies in the face of Scripture. Ultimately, the "anguish of being" experienced by the existentialist, be he theistic or atheistic, is derived from a misunderstanding of ultimate reality, or the misunderstanding of the being which is God-being, and how it is separated from human-being because of human sin.

Olson defined the existential "anguish before the here and now" as the anguish associated with the realization of the uniqueness of each person. Every individual exists for a brief period, in a minute volume of space that certainly appears insignificant considering the vastness of both time and space. Like the preceding description of the "anguish of being," this form of anguish is often resolved in Humanism by viewing the universe as eternal. The Greek Presocratic philosophers were pantheistic in their philosophy. They could not perceive of any reality that is transcendent from the universe. To address the concept of the eternal, the pantheist Spinoza coined the Latin phrase, *sub specie aeternitatis*, which implies the necessity of looking outside of time and space, i.e., looking to the eternal, for resolution of that concept which is the existential "anguish before the here and now." The pantheistic solution seems to be coming increasingly in vogue to refute the scientific evidence which points to the universe as having a beginning point in time. A universe with a beginning precludes any concept of a pantheistic eternality as conceived by the Presocratic Greeks and Spinoza. Post-Socrates, Plato and Aristotle became aware of a transcendent reality which they incorrectly believed to be accessible solely through the intellect.

---

22. Olsen, *Intro to Existentialism*, 37.

Kierkegaard, the first existentialist, identified with the concept of existentialistic "anguish of before the here and now" despite his claim to Christian faith. Olson quoted from Kierkegaard's *Unscientific Postscript* to illustrate the point:

> Can the principle of mediation . . . help the existing individual? . . . The poor existing individual is confined to the straight-jacket of existence . . . How can it help to explain to a man how the eternal truth is to be understood eternally, when the supposed user of the explanation is prevented from so understanding it through being an existing individual, and merely become fantastic when he imagines himself to be *sub specie aeternitais*? What such a man needs instead is precisely an explanation of how the eternal truth is to be understood in determinations of time by one, who as existing, is himself in time, which even the worshipful Herr Professor concedes, if not always, at least once a quarter when he draws his salary.[23]

Kierkegaard's reference to "Herr Professor" refers to the German philosopher Georg Wilhelm Friedrich Hegel. As we will discuss in the chapter that focuses on Kierkegaard, their philosophies were at odds with each other even though both were coming from a Christian position. Note how Kierkegaard is sarcastically trying to pull "Herr Professor's" philosophy back into existential reality by referring to the simple reality of receiving a day's wage for a day's work. "Herr Professor's" philosophical endeavors became so complex that he forgot the average person, and that was, rightly, much to the chagrin of Kierkegaard. However, the existential anguish of which we are here discussing is resolved by one's ultimate relationship to the Judeo-Christian God, where the individual indeed becomes significant considering the eternal, as he or she brings glory to God through a changed nature which enables one to live a moral and upright life. Unfortunately, that concept becomes lost in Hegel's philosophy because of his obscure and rambling style. Nonetheless, Kierkegaard seems also to have missed that all-important connection between Jesus Christ and Christ's function as mediator between God and man.[24] Neither philosopher put enough emphasis on human separation from the Creator because of human sin.

Finally, in our consideration of existential anguish, we will look at the said "anguish of freedom." As pointed out by Olson, the "anguish of freedom" obviously cannot mean that one experiences anguish due to the

---

23. Olsen, *Intro to Existentialism*, 43.

24. 1 Tim 2:5.

freedom of choice which may lead to the completion of a desired goal. This is especially true if one has the means to make any of several choices that may lead to the fulfillment of that goal. For example, there is no true anguish associated with the freedom to choose between a Porsche or a Ferrari, or any one of many other fine automotive choices, in satisfying one's wish for a high-performance sports car if one has the means to make the purchase. However, a more proper illustration of the anguish of existential choice would be the example of the senior graduating from high school who must at once choose to enter the work force, or choose to join the military, or choose to enter a trade school, or choose to become a gambler, or choose to try her hand at higher education, or simply choose to get married and have children. There is a definite anguish of freedom experienced by such an individual because she cannot *not* choose. By not choosing any choice she has made a choice which will have its own consequences. Thus, for the existentialist the concept of the "anguish of freedom" is the defining principle that results in the most destructive idea of Existentialism. As stated by Olson:

> The relationship between the anguish of being and the anguish of freedom is also reciprocal. In rough and general terms it can be put this way: To the extent that man is free, it is by his choices of decisions that the natural and social world become meaningful . . . It follows from this that in so far as a man is conscious of his freedom, his natural and social environment will take on the character of a brute fact, something contingent, absurd, alien; for consciousness of freedom is also consciousness of the fact that meaning comes to being through us.[25]

And, thus, in the concept of anguish is the defining destructive characteristic of the entire movement of Existentialism. In Existentialism every individual is responsible for defining his own individual meaning and purpose for living. Furthermore, whatever that meaning and purpose may be for any given individual, it is inherently the correct meaning and purpose for that individual, and as such that meaning and purpose can never be challenged regarding its legitimacy. But, of course, such a philosophy is absolutely opposed to Scripture. The only true source for anyone to discover their true meaning and purpose is found in Scripture. True meaning and purpose can come only when one finds them in relationship to his or her creator. True meaning and purpose are never found in one's own existence but in

25. Olsen, *Intro to Existentialism*, 52–53.

understanding one's existence in relationship to the existence of the creator of all things, i.e., the source of absolute existence. Furthermore, it is important to note that it is in the idea that every existing individual is responsible for defining his own meaning and purpose that has led to the belief in the relativity of truth, i.e., the idea that there are no absolute truths. If every person is responsible for defining his or her own meaning and purpose, then what is true and meaningful for you may not be true and meaningful to me. If believing that Hare Krishna is the source of ultimate reality for you, then that is what is real because it works for you. Anyone who knows the Postmodern mindset understands this is the overwhelming source of error that popular thought has perpetrated on the contemporary mind.

With this brief introduction to the subject of Existentialism, in the next chapter we will discuss the transition from the Humanism of the Modern era to the Humanism of our contemporary Postmodern era that follows from this existentialistic philosophy. Then in chapters 3, 4, and 5, we consider the lives, and some teachings, of the pioneering existentialists, Kierkegaard, Sartre, and Jaspers, who may be respectively classified as religious, secular, and Non-Secular existentialists.

2
_____

The Transition from Enlightenment Modern Humanism to Postmodern Existential Humanism

THE WELL-KNOWN SAYING THAT "history repeats itself" is true because human nature is the same today as it has always been. In Greek philosophy are observed some of the same cycles of human thought that are seen in more contemporary settings. In this chapter we will first briefly review the transition from Presocratic to Sophistic thought which occurred in ancient Greek philosophy. This transition has some parallels to the transition from the Humanism of the Modern era to the Existentialism of our contemporary Postmodern era, which is currently in progress. In both cases are observed a period where there existed significant philosophical uncertainty as to the role and nature of deity in understanding ultimate reality and a situation where that uncertainty resulted in the conclusion that absolute truth, particularly truth concerning moral absolutes, is impossible to know. Then we will reconsider some history of the Modern Humanism which was the primary focus of my earlier book and then consider some preliminary aspects of the transition from that Modern Humanism to the Postmodern Humanism which is the subject of the present book.

The Transition from Presocratic Philosophy to Sophistic Existentialism

The rich tradition in ancient Greek mythology stemmed from the Greek desire to understand and explain ultimate reality. However, mythology brought no real understanding to that lofty goal. As a result, formal Greek philosophy is said to have begun with the Presocratic philosophers, i.e., the philosophers who directly preceded Socrates. The Presocratic philosophers became noted for their worldviews which were pantheistic in character. Thales of the sixth century BC was the first ancient Greek philosopher to try to understand reality without resorting to myths, fantasies, and superstition, as did those who came before him. To put his era into a timeframe that the reader might better identify with, Thales was living in Miletus at the time of the Babylonian invasion of Judea and the later exile of the Jews to Babylon. Thales was then a contemporary of the Hebrew prophet Daniel. Thales, and the many Presocratic philosophers who came after him, had an intuitive understanding that something more significant than observable phenomenology, i.e., observable natural processes, was responsible for the whole of phenomenological reality.

Into the philosophical debate that swarmed around the nature of the pantheism of the Presocratic philosophers came the Sophists. Their philosophy developed because of their opposition to the faulty, and often conflicting, pantheistic beliefs of the Presocratic philosophers.[1] As a result, the Sophists proclaimed that absolute truth did not exist. According to them truth was relative to a given situation. Thus, education in rhetoric became a priority because they believed that the ones most skilled in debate were the ultimate determiners of reality.[2] Protagoras, the best known of the ancient Greek Sophists, notoriously proclaimed that "*man is the measure of all things*." Sophistic atheistic Humanism was thus actually a form of the existentialistic Humanism with which this present work is concerned. The denial of absolute truth became a defining principle in the conception of the Sophistic outlook of reality. In other words, the Humanism of our Postmodern era, with its refusal to acknowledge the existence of absolute truth, particularly concerning moral knowledge, is a repeat of Western history.

Plato, the noted student of Socrates, destroyed the arguments of the Sophists rather succinctly by pointing out that if truth were a relative proposition or simply a product of opinion, then for anyone to believe that truth is absolute would negate the possibility that truth could be relative.[3]

1. Carter, *Western Humanism*, 2–19.

2. An excellent example that demonstrates particularly well how superior rhetoric skills can lead to deadly error is nowhere more apparent than in the case of Germany's Hitler. Hitler was a master rhetorician and was able to persuade an entire nation to an ideology that ultimately led to its destruction.

3. Sahakian, *Great Philosophers*, 153.

Thus, because the existentialistic Humanism of the Sophists failed to acknowledge the existence of absolute truth, the Non-Secular Humanism of Socrates, Plato and Aristotle—based in the authority of human reason—became a foundational tenet of Western philosophy, and continued in that role until Postmodern Existentialism began to exert its influence in the midst of the twentieth century. Unfortunately, however, Plato and Aristotle *wrongly* taught that human nature was bent towards the good and that morality could be arrived at through the proper functioning of the reasoning intellect. This is the worldview that exalts human reason as the absolute means by which ultimate reality is perceived. This thinking gave rise to the Humanism of the Enlightenment. While Enlightenment philosophy began with deistic beliefs, it ended in a scientific rationalism which gradually progressed into the Secular Humanism of the Modern era.

The Secular Humanism of the Modern Era

The unprecedented successes of science fueled the idealism of the Enlightenment and subsequently ushered in the Modern era. In my earlier book, when focusing on the key features of the Enlightenment, I discussed the philosophies of Voltaire, Kant, and some of the leaders of the American version of the Enlightenment, namely Thomas Jefferson and Benjamin Franklin. All these influential thinkers acquiesced to the existence of a supreme being. However, based upon the content of their writings, it is probable that not even one of these influential leaders had a genuine relationship with the God of Scripture, i.e., Jesus, the Christ. As I pointed out in my earlier book, even Immanuel Kant— whose philosophy went to the greatest depth of all the Enlightenment thinkers, particularly in regards to moral philosophy— was seriously lacking in his understanding of the imputed righteousness imparted by Jesus to the individual who turns to him for eternal life. In that book I showed how Kant specifically taught that the driving force behind moral action was duty and not inclination. Yet it is the spiritual new birth (and the imputed righteousness that comes through that new birth) that is responsible for inclining the will towards genuine moral action. As the whole history of Israel has proven, a sense of duty to the law has never produced genuine moral transformation.[4] It was the Non-Secular Humanism of the Enlightenment that eventually gave way to the Secular Humanism of the Modern era. The deistic god of the Enlightenment was a false god,

4. Carter, *Western Humanism*, 126–33.

and the scientific mind will always be inclined to atheism in preference to believing in a god that it perceives as not real. Thus, the philosophical focus of the Enlightenment proceeded from a deistic system to one of atheism.

In my earlier book, when introducing the subject of the pantheism which characterized the bulk of Presocratic Greek thought, I quoted from Professor Robert Flint's book *Anti-Theistic Theories*. For a fresh look at the Secular Humanism that proceeded from the Enlightenment, I will here again make use of this work. Flint was a professor of theology and moral philosophy, during a period coinciding with that of the Modern era, at the then quite prestigious University of Edinburgh. *Anti-Theistic Theories* was published in 1879, i.e., at about the same time that the ideas of Darwin were first becoming established in Western systems of higher education.[5] Darwin's *The Origin of Species* had been in print for less than 20 years at the time of the 1877 Baird Lectures. (*Anti-Theistic Theories* is based upon those lectures.)

Although the work is now obscure, Professor Flint's *Anti-Theistic Theories* is still significant for two primary reasons. First, Modern Secular Humanism with its emphasis on either denying or doubting God's existence, based on Darwin's teachings, is a product of Western European culture. As a European professor of theology and philosophy at a premier European university, Flint had firsthand knowledge of the secular philosophies that were then coming out of the major European universities. Therefore, *Anti-Theistic Theories* is a firsthand account of the secular atheistic teachings that were becoming popular during the closing years of the nineteenth century. Flint's work serves as a first accounting to the extent that those teachings were to adversely affect Modern Western culture. Professor Flint had a keen awareness of the significance of Darwin's work. He correctly foresaw the important implications of Darwin's *The Origin of Species* in moving Western worldviews from Christianity to Modern Secular Humanism. Secondly, *Anti-Theistic Theories* is significant because of its contributions to Christian apologetics at a time when biblical-based Western thinking was first being seriously challenged in academia. This work of Flint appeared just prior to the height of the thinking that brought Secular Humanism into prominence.

---

5 The criticism of evolution, wherever it occurs in this volume, does not include the observable evolution within a species that are obvious valid mechanisms of adaptation. However, that criticism is indeed aimed at the idea that those same mechanisms can account for the evolution of human life from atoms of carbon, oxygen, hydrogen, phosphorous, and nitrogen. Those ideas, I maintain to be mere speculation of which there is absolutely no scientific proof.

Early on in *Anti-Theistic Theories*, Flint acknowledged that many people make the claim that a genuine atheist cannot truly exist. Flint wrote:

> The existence of atheism has often been doubted. It has been held to be absolutely impossible for a man entirely to throw off belief in God. The thought of a universe without a creator, without a presiding mind and sustaining will, without a judge of right and wrong, has seemed to man to be so incredible that they have refused to admit that it could be sincerely entertained by the human mind.[6]

While sympathetic to this viewpoint, and even giving a degree of support for such thinking, Flint nonetheless ultimately acknowledged that an atheist could be sincere in his belief of the non-existence of God. Flint, however, noted that very few atheists have ever attempted to prove their claim. Most all thinking people, atheists included, have the intelligence to know that such proof is impossible. Flint wrote:

> It is proverbially difficult to prove a negative, and there can be no negative so difficult to prove as that there is no God. Were a man to be landed on an unknown island, the print of a foot, a shell, a feather . . . would be sufficient to show him that some living creature had been there; but he would require to traverse the whole island, and examine every nook and corner, every object and every inch of space in it, before he was entitled to affirm that no living creature had been there.[7]

Flint held that the inroads to materialistic atheism in England were put in check by the likes of Ralph Cudworth, Thomas More, Isaac Newton, Robert Boyle, Samuel Clarke, and Thomas Sherlock. But France, having persecuted many of her Protestant converts, did not enjoy those same biblical influences to stave off these same humanistic inroads. The culture of France, at least for the most part, was not friendly to the true gospel of Christ during the period that the Reformation in Germany was changing the course of European Christianity. Luther wrote (in his *Table Talks*) concerning the martyrdom that Protestants were then experiencing in France, "We are sheep for the slaughter. Only the other day, they burned, at Paris, two nobles and two magistrates, victims in the cause of the gospel, the king himself (Francis I), setting fire to the faggots."[8] According to Flint,

6. Flint, *Anti-Theistic*, 5.

7. Flint, *Anti-Theistic*, 9.

8. Luther, *Table Talks*, 66.

in France, the French Revolution brought a retarding influence to materialistic atheism, but the extraordinary successes of science and technology, which began soon afterward, again brought about its re-ignition. Writing in the present tense, Flint observed:

> Materialism has gained to itself a lamentably large proportion of the chiefs of contemporary science, and it finds in them advocates as outspoken and enthusiastic as were Lucretius and Holbach. Multitudes are disposed to listen and believe with an uninquiring and irrational faith. Materialism—atheistical materialism—may at no distant date, unless earnestly and wisely opposed, be strong enough to alter all our institutions, and to abolish those which it dislikes.[9]

Therefore, Flint foresaw the considerable influence of science in general, and Darwin's work in particular, towards the rise of Secular Humanism in Western culture, although he did not live to see the full impact of Darwin's writing.[10] When specifically predicting the negative impact of Darwin's work, Flint wrote:

> Three generations of Darwins have entertained materialistic convictions. Works like Thomas Hope's 'Essay on the Origin and Progress of Man,' and the anonymous 'Vestiges of Creation,' connect the 'Zoonomia' of Erasmus Darwin with the 'Origin of Species' of Charles Darwin.[11]

It is well known that Charles Darwin's theory of evolution, which touted the mechanism of natural selection to account for the generation of species, has been the pivotal work which has equipped the materialistic atheist with his false justification for throwing off all belief in a supernatural creator.

While Flint did not live long enough to see firsthand the mature development of Secular Humanism in Western culture, he foresaw hints of that development. Recalling that the philosophy of the ancient Greek Sophists (which grew out of the Pantheism of the Presocratic philosophers) has strong parallels to Western Postmodern developments (i.e., the atheistic

---

9. Flint, *Anti-Theistic*, 99–100.

10. In this chapter, I use the term Secular Humanism interchangeably with Flint's terminology, materialistic atheism. As before noted, many Enlightenment humanists were not atheistic per se, but the ultimate outcome of the Humanism proceeding from the Enlightenment was indeed one of atheism. It should be noted that even Non-Secular Humanism is essentially materialistic because of its failure to fully comprehend the spiritual nature of ultimate reality.

11. Flint, *Anti-Theistic*, 100. (*Vestiges of Creation* was authored by Robert Chambers.).

Sophists were primarily existentialistic humanists in that they denied the concept of absolute truth) it is interesting to note that Flint commented on the Humanism of Augusta Comte, the French humanist who was contemporary with him. While Comte gave his teachings the term Positivism,[12] Flint stated that "It [i.e., Comte's philosophy] was taught in all its essential principles by Protagoras and others in Greece more than four hundred years before the Christian era. Positivism is the phenomenalism of the Greek Sophists revived and adapted to the demands of the present age."[13] And as stated by Sahakian and Sahakian, "Comte's Humanism postulated love as its principle, order as its basis, and progress as its aim; it was a kind of religion without theology, an ethics substituted for dogma."[14] However, Professor Flint lived about ten years into the twentieth century, and thus he witnessed his prophecy regarding the alteration of Western educational and religious institutions begin to be fulfilled. Ironically, any current day educator with the belief system of Flint would find it most difficult, if not impossible, to gain a teaching position in any of the prestigious schools of Western culture because of the respect that Secular Humanism still commands in academia. While Darwin's work was steadily gaining acceptance at the time *Anti-Theistic Theories* was published, those atheistic materialists who built on Darwin's ideas, were yet to formulate the teachings which would propel modern Secular Humanism into the limelight of academic thinking.

The Onset of Postmodern Existentialism

Secular Humanism, however, which holds to an epistemology posited solely in science, has not developed into the primary belief system of contemporary Western culture, despite that it still is highly influential in Western academia. The Modern Humanism which evolved from Enlightenment thinking, where reason reigned supreme in the human quest for meaning and purpose, has given way to the individualism of Postmodernism Existentialism. While the ideal of moral advancement in Modern Humanism is focused more on society as a whole and less so on the individual, that model of morality breaks down because morality must begin with the individual which then will yield positive repercussions in society.

12. Although Positivism largely equates with Western Secular Humanism, Flint specifically linked it to the philosophy of the ancient Sophists.

13. Flint, *Anti-Theistic*, 177.

14. Sahakian, *Great Philosophers*, 153.

The Secular humanistic ideal where positive law is used to affect change in human nature fails because human nature is never turned towards true moral wholeness—i.e., the moral wholeness, or righteousness, which must be imputed by God—through human effort.

A close examination of Western thought reveals that at the end of the Second World War, the Modern worldview began to slowly transition back to an existentialistic Sophistic type of worldview. In other words, belief in the existence of absolute truth began to lose traction in the Western mind about midway through the twentieth century. Perceptions of reality over a period of a few years became primarily based in image and opinion—and in the supremacy of an imagined freedom of human will.

When the concept of absolute truth goes by the wayside, perceptions of reality can easily become based in falsehood, and this is the phenomenon that we are currently seeing on a grand scale in Western culture. As the writer of Proverbs so well put it, "There is a way which seems right to a man/ But its end is the way of death."[15] I was recently driving in an unfamiliar city when I came upon a billboard that at once reminded me of this informative verse of Scripture. The billboard read, "Imagine getting fired because of who you love." The message was obviously sponsored by a pro-homosexual organization, and it was obviously making an appeal to a "way which seems right." But just as the Proverbs reminds us, there are ways which seem to appeal to a concept of good, but the end of those ways results in death. A homosexual lifestyle, or a lifestyle of adulterous living, might appeal to many as being amoral, but those lifestyles will certainly result in eternal separation from everlasting life—they are lifestyles which will lead to certain eternal separation from God, i.e., eternal death. Likewise, even though the majority of those who make up contemporary Postmodern Western culture may perceive that there are many ways that lead to knowledge of ultimate reality, i.e., the God who imparts eternal life, those perceptions are not based in truth, and they too will lead to eternal damnation. Jesus declared with authority: "I am the way, and the truth, and the life; no one comes to the Father but through Me."[16]

Because Existentialism results in a subjective worldview, there are those humanists who are making significant attempts to bring Humanism back to its Modern Secular moorings.[17] At one point in Modern Western

15. Prov 14:12.

16. John 14:6.

17. For a primary example see Grayling, *The God Argument: The Case Against Religion and for Humanism.*

culture, it appeared that atheistic Secular Humanism, particularly in Western educational systems, might completely triumph over any worldview that acknowledges the reality of the supernatural, i.e., the transcendent Creator of Scripture. However, the onset of Existentialism (even though Existentialism has its own brand of atheism as is seen in the atheism of Sartre) has contributed to blunting the triumph of that Secular atheism based in Enlightenment science, which sees the whole of reality as only that which is contained within the material universe, i.e., naturalism. But despite the rise of Postmodern Existentialism, Secular Humanism, of course, still maintains a strong presence in Western culture, particularly so in academia. This fact explains, to a significant extent, why the humanistic Postmodern existentialistic mindset has been slow to be acknowledged as a substantial and influential movement in Western thought. The fact that Postmodern Existentialism is still not universally acknowledged, particularly in systems of Christian education, sometimes gives the illusion that the Modern mindset, based in the authority of science, is wielding more power in controlling the formation of worldviews than it does.

The two primary philosophers, whose ideas were of primary importance in this movement to Postmodern Existentialism, were the German Friedrich Nietzsche and the Dane Søren Kierkegaard. Although I noted in my prior book how Nietzsche took the emphasis that Western philosophy had traditionally placed on human reason and shifted it to human will, I did not specifically identify his philosophy as a primary stepping stone in the transition to the Postmodern era, and this oversight was not with intention. Furthermore, I failed in my earlier book to introduce my reader to the writings of the Danish Kierkegaard, who, although Christian in his profession, was instrumental in bringing Existentialism to prominence in the Postmodern mind. Professor Flint did not address the work of either Nietzsche or Kierkegaard, but this should not be too surprising since the notoriety of either of them had not yet been established. (Both philosophers were contemporary with Flint.) However, as the writings of Nietzsche and Kierkegaard became more widely published, both posthumously, their ideas were especially instrumental in shifting the emphasis in Western humanistic philosophy from *reason* to *volition* and, thus, from Modern to Postmodern ideology. Nietzsche specifically sought to praise the ancient Sophists for their de-emphasis of human reason in lieu of the classical Greek philosophers who were responsible for pointing out to the

Sophists their error in not acknowledging the existence of absolute truth.[18] Kierkegaard likewise, in opposition to the influence of Hegel, sought to turn away from the prevalence of human reason in Western culture and instead sought the primacy of human volition. In other words, Kierkegaard viewed human volition as the primary means for the self-determination of human destiny. In the chapters which follow we will continue to stress that the precedent in Postmodernism is the formation of a worldview which emphasizes the rejection of the concept of absolute truth—and the acceptance of the subjective freedom of human will—in lieu of fact and reason. The Postmodern humanistic mind therefore holds to a faulty view of reality because in this system of thought, image and opinion take precedence over fact and reason.

Another primary reason that the shift from Modernism to Postmodernism is often not immediately evident, is that those in academia who have gained extraordinary popular fame and claim to be operating in a scientific rational mindset are in reality operating in an existentialistic mindset even though they might be doing so without full knowledge of that fact.[19] Two primary, famous academicians in Western culture who fit into this category are the late Professor Carl Sagan of Cornell University (who when introducing his series "Cosmos" in 1980, boldly proclaimed: "The Cosmos is all that is or was or ever will be.") and Professor Richard Dawkins of Oxford University, who is currently the most prolific spokesperson for atheistic Darwinian evolution in the world today.

When I reflect on the career of Sagan, it is difficult for me to acknowledge him as an outstanding scientist, despite the fame he acquired. I have often wondered if his well-known fondness for marijuana might have triggered in him the many bizarre ideas that to me seem to border on pseudoscience. He possessed a mind which ran wild with unrealistic imaginations, and possibly created many of the hypotheses which at best could be described as approaching the irrational.[20] Early on in his career, he entertained the possibility that unidentified flying objects (UFOs) could

18. Carter, *Western Humanism*, 154.

19. I will provide an outstanding example of this in chapter 8 with the example of a debate between Professor William Lane Craig and the scientist Dr. Begon. Begon is not well known outside of his scientific discipline, but this example shows particularly well the point that I am making here. While Begon ostensibly argued from a scientific standpoint, in practicality his arguments were thoroughly existentialistic.

20. It is well known that Sagan was denied tenure at Harvard, and that may have been due to his propensity for putting forth the ideas to which I here refer.

very well be genuine visitations of life-forms originating in outer space, although probably for the sake of maintaining an appearance of legitimacy, he eventually expressed doubt that the many claimed UFOs sightings could represent genuine visitations from other worlds. Nonetheless, Sagan's propensity for believing that aliens from distant galaxies were a reality never completely abated, as he was one of the main players in the organization known as SETI, (Search for Extraterrestrial Intelligence), an organization that has spent millions of dollars in trying to communicate with imagined intelligent life forms from within the cosmos. SETI is still active in sending radio signals into deep outer space with the hope of communicating with some form of life, the expectations of which have little genuine basis. Of course, all experimental scientists have formed hypotheses which have yielded negative results, including myself. But any experiment which continually yields negative outcomes should eventually lead the scientist to conclude that either the experimental design is faulty or that a new hypothesis is needed. Most rational minds would have, by now, concluded that there are no intelligent life forms in outer space who are receiving or sending radio signals. Would not it be more reasonable to divert the millions being spent on such futile research to more promising work? Is it really any wonder why Enlightenment Humanism is losing ground to the Postmodern worldview based on the irrational claims being made in the name of science?

After Iraqi forces invaded Kuwait in August of 1990, Sadam Hussein threatened to set his oil fields on fire if he was opposed by U.N. forces. In response, Professor Sagan, who often became involved in political issues, proclaimed that such an event would yield the devastating effects of a nuclear winter. But Sagan's prediction proved to be false when Hussein lit up the fields. Perhaps because of that faulty projection, Dr. Sagan was shortly thereafter rejected for membership in the National Academy of Sciences.[21] But the point to take away from these observations is the fact that no one should be surprised that many claims made in the name of science are losing the respect of the general population and are, thus, promoting the Postmodern worldview which rejects reason over a preference to volition. When a scientist makes the proclamation that "the cosmos is all there is," the postmodern mind simply shrugs off that claim as being mere opinion, and because there is no such thing as absolute truth, either accepts or rejects that contention. A scientist should never make claims in the name of

21. Morrison, "Carl Sagan's Life," 29–36.

science that are not subject to the proof of science. Any scientist should be purporting only that which is factual and rational and which can be shown to be so by reproducible experimental evidence. Sagan was an existential Postmodern philosopher affecting Postmodern minds by reinforcing the Postmodern contention that there is no such thing as absolute truth.

In the example of Oxford's Richard Dawkins, a similar scenario unfolds. Dawkins is exceedingly vocal in his opposition to anyone who holds to a view of ultimate reality based in the knowledge of the transcendent God of Scripture. He seems to get great satisfaction in portraying those as ignorant who believe that the supernatural Hebrew account of creation, as revealed to Moses, supplies the framework for a proper understanding of the birth of the cosmos. Of course, in so doing, Dawkins has, not surprisingly, implied that the Apostle Paul was an ignoramus (as did Nietzsche), since the apostle clearly believed in the existence of an actual Adam. Dawkins is forced to deny the literal existence of the first human being, referred to in Scripture as Adam, because of his mistaken beliefs about the origin of man. Dawkins writes:

> All too many preachers, while agreeing that evolution is true and Adam and Eve never existed, will then blithely go into the pulpit and make some moral or theological point about Adam and Eve in their sermons without once mentioning that, of course, Adam and Eve never actually existed! If challenged, they will protest that they intended a purely 'symbolic' meaning, perhaps something to do with 'original sin', or the virtues of innocence.[22]

However, both Jesus and the Apostle Paul authenticated the truth of a literal Adam. But, of course, the declarations of both Jesus and the Apostle Paul have absolutely no impact in helping Dawkins understand the gravity of his error.[23] Dawkins appears to be particularly frustrated, knowing that many people in Western culture, even those with high degrees of education, yet show at least a degree of respect to individuals who believe in the existence of the transcendent personal deity of Hebrew and Greek Scripture. But to show that Dawkins is working more from Postmodern volition than from the Enlightenment reason he wishes to portray, it would be useful to contrast his Darwinism to the evolutionary beliefs of his Harvard colleague, namely the late Steven Jay Gould. It is well known that a long-standing debate between the two evolutionists dominated academic

22. Dawkins, *Greatest Show*, 7–8.
23. Matt 19:3–5, Rom 5:14, 1 Cor 15:22.

biology for many years. Professor Gould held to a theory of evolution which is more in-line with most of the existing fossil record.[24] Those Christians, many of whom are qualified professional biologists, who have opposed the theory of Darwinian evolution, which teaches that the origin of species came about through gradual evolution over a period of 14 billion years, have clearly pointed out that the existing fossil record does not support that theory of gradual change to which Dawkins holds. However, despite the clear rational evidence of the fossil record, Dawkins holds to his theory, and falsely claims it as proven fact. Clearly Dawkins's will to believe the irrational has taken precedence over what is real, and as I emphasize throughout this work, the placement of volition over reason is a primary characteristic of Postmodern existentialism.

Why Theology Will Always Matter in Matters of Philosophy

When the entire history of Western philosophy is considered, it should be understandable how the Postmodern worldview has evolved into the reality it is today. Philosophy is intimately linked to the subject of theology, and it is therefore impossible to probe into either philosophy or theology without touching on the other for the simple reason that both subjects are primarily concerned with gaining an understanding of what is ultimately real. As the ancient Greek Presocratic philosophers attempted to gain an understanding of ultimate reality, theology entered their worldview in the form of pantheism. The Presocratics believed that ultimate reality was contained within nature, and they sought to understand it by reaching for a knowledge of that nature. The Sophists came on the scene primarily in opposition to the Presocratics. They were accepted as practical philosophers because they opposed that pantheistic worldview which they intuitively, and correctly, perceived as a wrong interpretation of reality. However, they could not conceive of a transcendent ultimate reality, and thus the only reality in the Sophist's worldview was that which could be at once perceived by the senses. The Sophists maintained that physical nature could never be completely understood. As such, they were only concerned with understanding human nature, in a secular sense, over any desire to understand the nature of the universe and the "gods" who may have been responsible for the origin of that universe. Hence, as I pointed earlier, the worldview of

24. Gould advocated the idea of "punctuated equilibrium" to better account for the actualities of the fossil record.

the Sophists became existentialistic in scope. In denying the possibility that absolute truth of ultimate reality could ever be known with certainty, the Sophists were forced to put the subject of morality into a humanistic existential relative vein. Whenever a transcendent ultimate reality is excluded in any worldview, a humanistic understanding of morality is mandated. Therefore, the sophistic tradition evolved into a view where moral relativity was paramount and where every man did what was right in his own eyes.

This reality, of course, reflects the pattern seen in the existentialistic worldview of our contemporary Postmodern environment. In Postmodern Humanism there is a tendency to put less emphasis on knowledge of the outside world, i.e., in a desire for genuine scientific endeavor, in favor of a worldview which sees the primary importance as that which concerns immediate consciousness. That worldview has led to an interest in a science that caters more to naturalistic philosophical speculation than it does to a genuine affirmation of natural truth. The understanding of nature that results solely from reproducible experimentation should be the only goal of science. And along with the shift from an interest in scientific knowledge to an interest in the self's existence is the shift in the emphasis on *rational* thought to that of merely satisfying individual desires through sheer willpower. The ultimate result of this, especially in the sciences of biology and cosmology, is the declaration of "facts" which are only mere speculation, or worse, only wishful thinking.

It is because of God's transcendence that knowledge of himself requires revelation. Without revelation, the human capacity for discovery of all knowledge that is transcendent to the universe is impossible. Of course, because of the necessity of special revelation, theology cannot entirely stand by itself in the realm of reason. But at the same time, knowledge that comes by either natural or special revelation does not stand apart from reason.[25] Acknowledgment of this fact is perhaps the greatest contribution of Plato to Western philosophy.[26] However, Greek philosophy was handicapped by its Pre-Christian roots. The special revelation for knowledge of ultimate reality was then confined to the Jew. By the time Greek philosophy had matured, the Jewish people, in the main, had rejected their God, as is clear

25. An obvious example of natural revelation is the fact that the observed complexity of nature itself demands intelligent purpose. In Scripture an example of natural revelation, given through special revelation, is Psalm 19:1 which reads, "*The heavens declare the glory of God and the firmament showeth forth his handiwork.*"

26. With Plato's *Theory of Forms*, the concept of a transcendent ultimate reality, apart from special revelation, was made compatible with reason.

by both the content of Malachi's prophecy, and by the fact that they rejected their Messiah who was revealed soon afterwards. Malachi, the last of the Hebrew prophets before the advent of Jesus, was contemporary with Plato. As a result of that rejection, special written revelation to the Hebrew people was thus in its final stages. The apostle Paul, whom God supernaturally chose to bring the knowledge of ultimate reality to the Gentiles (i.e., the gospel), in his writing to the Romans, stated that the Jews had once been in a privileged position because to them had been committed the special revelation of the "oracles of God."[27] Thus, Greek philosophy prepared the Western Gentile mind for the acceptance of the reality of a transcendent God, a concept that mind had previously found difficult to comprehend. Unfortunately, however, the Western mind has traditionally given preference to the authority of pure stand-alone reason. In his writing to the Greeks of Corinth, the Apostle Paul put the wisdom of secular thinking, which is based purely on human reason, in perspective with the wisdom that brings about a saving knowledge of ultimate reality. Paul writes:

> For the word of the cross is foolishness to those who are perishing, but to us who are being saved it is the power of God. For it is written, "I will destroy the wisdom of the wise, And the cleverness of the clever I will set aside." Where is the wise man? Where is the scribe? Where is the debater of this age? Has not God made foolish the wisdom of the world? For since in the wisdom of God the world through its wisdom did not come to know God, God was well-pleased through the foolishness of the message preached to save those who believe. For indeed Jews ask for signs and Greeks search for wisdom; but we preach Christ crucified, to Jews a stumbling block and to Gentiles foolishness, but to those who are the called, both Jews and Greeks, Christ the power of God and the wisdom of God. Because the foolishness of God is wiser than men, and the weakness of God is stronger than men.[28]

As Christianity progressed in Western culture, it again fell into the error of exalting human reason over special revelation. Thomas Aquinas, sought to make church doctrine compatible with the humanistic philosophy of Aristotle, and church doctrine became shaped more by the philosophy of Scholasticism than by the revelation of Scripture. It took the Reformers to put church doctrine back into a proper relationship with

27. Rom 3:2.
28. 1 Cor 1:18–25.

Scripture. But with the onset of the Enlightenment, human reason was not only exalted again over the revelation of Scripture, but all revelation that did not appear compatible with naturalism was completely rejected, and Christianity found itself in the cross-hairs of the humanistic mindset which sought to divorce the reality of the transcendent God of Hebrew and Greek Scripture from being taught as fact in all venues of Western education, and that Enlightenment Humanism spilled over into the Christian church. The German led movement of the so-called Higher Criticism of the nineteenth century sought to strip Scripture of its supernatural special revelation, and that movement was eventually highly effective at weakening the message of the gospel in the mainline Protestant churches of the West during the late nineteenth and early twentieth centuries. While the Enlightenment advanced the cause of science (which is rightfully based on the authority of reason) science unfortunately became entangled in philosophical subjects where it had no rightful authority. *Science cannot be used to prove or deny the reality of the transcendent God.*

Therefore, when naturalism became the primary philosophy of Western educational systems, science became exalted as the only means for the interpretation of all reality. But in so doing, Western educational systems turned prevailing worldviews back to the irrational. The rational mind, simply from perceiving the reality of the awe-inspiring beauty and complexity of the universe and the life which it maintains, learns of God's necessary existence. The natural revelation of God's existence is the reason, as the Apostle declared to the Romans, that all will be held without excuse for the responsibility of acknowledging the existence of the one true transcendent God.[29] Western educational systems are, therefore, ultimately responsible for bringing back to the Western mind the Postmodern condition that refuses to acknowledge the existence of absolute truth, which is the very condition that existed in the early Greek systems of education that came into existence with the ancient Greek Sophists. Plato gained notoriety because he was able to show the gross error in Sophistic thinking.

While the Secular Humanism derived from Enlightenment ideology may yet today dominate certain sectors of the secular academic world, that ideal—which looks to be based solely in human reason—becomes based more on human will. When any rational evidence is introduced that points to error in the evolutionary worldview which denies the existence of God, the Postmodern mind believes it is free to dismiss that evidence.

29. Rom 1:20.

The Postmodern mind simply wills that evidence will not alter its thinking, not caring if a given proposition is true or not, if it conflicts with its fixed worldview—because absolute truth, especially truth that involves anything transcendent to the universe, cannot be determined, according to Postmodern thinking. In other words, when the Postmodern mind ignores the natural revelation of nature and the special revelation of Scripture, both of which give sufficient evidence for God's existence, that mind feels justified in holding on to its atheistic or agnostic worldview since the question of God's existence, according to the Postmodern worldview, cannot be known. To the Postmodern mind, absolute truth does not exist, especially in the arena of the metaphysical. The Postmodern mind simply wills to ignore any evidence that goes against what it wills to believe, and reason is tossed aside.

The Postmodern Attitude Towards Science

While I concentrate in chapter 7 on reviewing the malpractice which often occurs in Postmodern Science, I here put into perspective how the Postmodern non-scientific mind often judges the subject of science, be it legitimate science or so-called, illegitimate, science. There should be little wonder that the Postmodern populace holds more to a worldview which wills to refuse truth, be it scientific or scriptural truth. The existentialist mind simply chooses not to accept what it does not wish to accept. This chapter closes with an example that demonstrates how the existentialistic worldview has taken precedence over the worldview that was formed by Enlightenment Secular Humanism, despite the fact that Enlightenment Humanism is still dominant in academia. I give here another example to show how the Postmodern mind is indifferent to scientific authority, particularly when it conflicts with what the Postmodern mind wills to believe.

James D. Watson, co-discoverer of the double helical structure of DNA, is the quintessential example of a contemporary scientist who is still steeped in Enlightenment Humanism. Watson (who is still living at the time of this writing) is one of the most awarded scientists in the history of contemporary science. The list of accolades conferred upon him is indeed impressive. Watson is unapologetic in his atheism, taking pride in that position, as was pointed out in the summary chapter of my earlier book. But because of Watson's strong interest in the science of genetics, he has made numerous statements regarding inherited intelligence which many people have deemed to be racist because of the contemporary existential political climate—despite Watson's insistence that his position is backed up by rational data.[30] However, notwithstanding the notoriety to which Dr. Watson has attained as a world-renowned scientist, his statements regarding the subject of inherited intelligence are summarily rejected by the Postmodern humanistic mind without true consideration of their scientific merit—simply because the Postmodern mind does not dare to consider an intellectual position which might challenge the status-quo regarding what is considered to be politically correct.

Thus, the percentage of those who reject Christianity based on the authority of science is lower than what one might expect, given the prevalence of atheism in the science departments of the most prestigious Western institutions of higher learning. When the contemporary Postmodern mind rejects Christianity, it is more likely rejected because of the will to do so than because of any evidence from evolutionary science which has spilled over into the Postmodern era from so-called evolutionary science. Of course, when scientists authoritatively declare fossil ages that range in the millions to billions of years, based upon the sedimentary layers in which they are found, many non-critical thinking postmoderns buy into that line of thinking. However, because a worldwide flood did in fact occur, those sedimentary layers which geologists use to prove timelines of earth's history, of necessity, come into question. To assert that there is no evidence for a worldwide flood, which supports the scriptural contention of reality, is simply to bury one's head in the sand, as the popular metaphor describing willful ignorance goes. Rational minds who claim no particular allegiance to any religion should be able to understand the fact that if such a deluge did in fact happen, then the park rangers at Grand Canyon National Park, of necessity, would need to alter their information to those tourists who look to understand the awe-inspiring site before them. At any rate, it often becomes obvious to the Postmodern existentialistic mind that science can venture into areas where its authority is profoundly entrenched in uncertainty, if not in downright falsehood. When science is working as true science, it will bring to bear a view of reality that is not opposed to the revelation of Scripture—because of the truth of supernaturally inspired Scripture. Genuine science points to the fact that there was a point in time where time and space had a beginning. Secular science refers to this event as the "big bang," but Scripture refers to it as "In the beginning." Not surprisingly,

30. Rushton and Jensen, "Most Inconvenient Truth," 629–40.

contemporary secular humanistic scientists are diligently looking for a way out of acknowledging this convergence of truth to preserve a semblance of justification for their mistaken atheistic worldviews.

Although at the turn of the twentieth century Søren Kierkegaard had long passed from the scene due to a premature death, his pioneering existentialistic ideas, while in hibernation, were still very much alive. Existentialism would eventually pave the way for that Humanism which has become dominant in Postmodern Western culture, the era whose beginning is simultaneous with the beginning of my own life. In the final three chapters of Part 1 we will briefly probe into the lives and teachings of three of the more noteworthy Western existentialists, namely Søren Kierkegaard, Jean-Paul Sartre, and Karl Jaspers. While these existentialists varied in their beliefs about the existence of a transcendent ultimate reality, they nonetheless viewed reality as primarily characterized by existential experience with little regard to the human condition that separates human beings from the one true ultimate reality, i.e., the God of Holy Scripture. Kierkegaard, while a professed Christian, was the first to put Existentialism into the marketplace of ideas. On the other hand, Sartre was an unrepentant atheist who had no regard for anything outside of his immediate existence. Finally, Jaspers seemed to hold to a concept of the transcendent, but that concept was far removed from the God of Holy Scripture. Hopefully, the consideration of these three influential authors will help in understanding why Existentialism is gaining significance in Western culture and is vigorously opposing a worldview which is consistent with a scriptural interpretation of reality.

3

The Christian Existentialism of Kierkegaard

THE BIRTH OF EXISTENTIALISM is grounded in the work of Søren Kierkegaard (1813–1855). Kierkegaard was born in Copenhagen into a wealthy business family which allowed him a quality education. He was the youngest of seven children fathered by Michael Pederson Kierkegaard. He entered the University of Copenhagen in 1831, and about ten years later he received the Magister degree studying both theology and philosophy. At that time in the Danish educational system the Magister was equivalent to the current Western Doctor of Philosophy (PhD) degree. While still a student Kierkegaard embarked upon a writing career, but even after taking his degree he stayed an independent writer and remained aloof from any professional organizational affiliation. He lived an unconventional social life, which in large part birthed the uniqueness of his writing. One should, therefore, understand the environment in which he was raised, and found comfort in, to understand the thrust of his philosophy. It is important to note, in this context, that Kierkegaard's father had once confessed to Søren that because he had struggled as a young peasant he had once cursed God. The senior Kierkegaard believed this curse to have had a lingering negative effect on their immediate family. That belief may have come from the fact that most of Søren's siblings died prematurely. (Søren's brother, Peter, however, lived to age 82.) This knowledge had a profound effect on Søren, and much of his personality was shaped in coming to grips with the implications of this revelation. Although Kierkegaard's family was associated with the formal Danish state church, they also maintained ties with the more conservative and informal Moravian Brethren church.

That church was more closely identified with the agricultural classes left over from the feudal social system that had prevailed in Denmark before the establishment of its newly formed constitutional monarchy. Kierkegaard's father was originally from that rural culture, but his success in the textile industry had moved him into the circles of the higher social classes of Copenhagen culture, and thus the family became involved with the formal state church of Denmark.

Kierkegaard's Education

The major motivating force for the theological and philosophical direction of Kierkegaard's writing came from his association with those involved in his education at the University of Copenhagen. The university departments of theology and philosophy were, not surprisingly, in close alignment with the Danish state church. Because Hegelian philosophy in nineteenth century European culture became fashionable, university students of theology and philosophy were proficient in Hegelian thought, and this was particularly the case at the University of Copenhagen. That same Hegelian influence had spilled over into the Danish state church. The three major academic influences on the young Kierkegaard were Hans Martensen, Poul Møller, and Frederik Sibbern—all professors of theology/philosophy at the University of Copenhagen. Of these, Martensen was particularly a champion of Hegel, and he later became a bishop in the state church of Denmark. Because the philosophy of Hegel was so influential at the University of Copenhagen, to understand Kierkegaard, one must have at least an elementary understanding of Hegel. While Hegel's ideas have been appropriated by both genuine believers and atheists, there is no doubt that Hegel's philosophy has its foundations in Christianity. Hegel wrote with apparent sincerity, "Christ has appeared—a man who is God—God who is man; and thereby peace and reconciliation have accrued to the world."[1]

Unfortunately, however, Hegel's overall writing style is overbearingly obscure, and it takes much work to get to his ultimate philosophical conclusions. Nonetheless, it is well known that the primary influence of Hegel on Western thought is in his idea of the dialectic. Hegel taught that the cycle of discovering truth revolved around the ideas of the thesis and antithesis. According to Hegel, survey of the two extremes of any intellectual problem

---

1. Hegel, *Philosophy of History*, 306.

should be defined by a thesis which will always have present an opposing antithesis. The resolution of the thesis and antithesis should yield a position closer to the truth, i.e., the synthesis. Hegel's philosophical foundation in theology was the driving force for this aspect of his teaching, for which he is particularly famous. Anyone experienced in the intellectual problems of biblical theology should be able to identify the validity of Hegel's thought in the application of the dialectical argument which is attributed to him. For example, to put this dialectical concept into contemporary theological terms, one might view a "Hyper-Calvinist" as one whose beliefs regarding a supposed superior understanding of Calvin's teachings regarding human volition in the doctrine of salvation might represent the "thesis." The antithesis, of course, would be represented by the ideas of the staunch Armenian who, like the extreme Calvinist, has formed debatable views about the role of human volition in that same doctrine. According to Hegelian dialectical thought, there is a truth that resolves the primary issues of contention between these two extremes, referred to as "the synthesis." (And, importantly, the biblical view of the role of the human volition in salvation is, in fact, a synthesis of these two extremes, even though its understanding may be difficult to articulate.) However, with that said, this is another outstanding example of a point I emphasized in chapter 1 where I noted that in most all the noted philosophers of Western history one can usually discover an element of truth, no matter if the overall position of that philosopher is one of error. Professor Flint characterized Hegel's overall philosophical position as one of pantheism, and thus, as one that is incompatible with Scripture.[2]

It was Hegel's emphasis on human reason, and the abstractions it produced, that prompted Kierkegaard to become extremely critical of Hegel. In defense of Kierkegaard, there is no doubt that Hegel erred in not properly heeding the Apostle Paul's encouragement to the Christians at Colossae, to guard against the love of philosophical systems based upon human wisdom.[3] As a result of Kierkegaard's criticisms of Hegel, Kierkegaard and Martensen became enemies of each other, and it was, no doubt, the contention between the two that gave impetus for Kierkegaard's continued attack on the state church. Certainly, it appears that much of the tension between the state church and Kierkegaard involved a political element between these two personalities. Furthermore, it is probable that the birth of Kierkegaard's Existentialism was fueled by this animosity that existed

2. Flint, *Anti-Theistic*, 375–440.
3. Col 2:8.

between them. Another important person that figures into this contentious relationship between Martensen and Kierkegaard is J. L. Heiberg, a primary literary figure in Copenhagen society. Heiberg was a champion of Hegel, and he was primarily responsible for introducing the Hegelian influence into the Danish state church. Martensen was active in the Heiberg literary circle, and Kierkegaard had sought entrance into that circle. But Kierkegaard's efforts to join that literary group never met with success. There can be little doubt that Martensen was influential in preventing Kierkegaard from gaining entrance into that society, and that failure, no doubt, played a role in Kierkegaard's sense of rejection and isolation which contributed to his sense of alienation.[4]

It was under the influence of both Møller and Sibbern that Kierkegaard became immersed in the Romanticism that had developed as a backlash to the characteristic rationalism of the Enlightenment. Enlightenment rationalism had tended to downplay the "internal self-definition"[5] of the individual. As stated by Bukdahl:

> Internal self-definition means understanding oneself as an individual before relating to the many and to society. It means the excitement of feeling oneself supported by a rich inner world, a world saturated with fantasy and emotion though also saturated with Reason, which is something more than mere understanding.[6]

Møller and Sibbern, while primarily Christian in their thinking, sought to guard against the extremes to which this emphasis on individualism would eventually take their young student Kierkegaard. In Kierkegaard's concentration on individual existence, he lost sight of the whole of humanity. In *Mere Christianity* Lewis touched on many areas of Christian philosophy, and it should come as no surprise that he there addressed the individual from the perspective of the whole of humanity. Lewis thus dealt with the issue which is, in one sense, central to the entire subject of Existentialism. Here Lewis taught the necessity of understanding how the entire human race, in a sense, should be viewed as a single organism. And this fact, of course, is the reason that God has commanded the Christian to love his neighbor as himself. Therefore, individualism, as it regards the self, to prefer itself over the selves of others, is destructive in the quest for emotional contentment. Lewis stressed that if one forgets that his neighbor

4. McDonald, "Søren Kierkegaard."
5. Bukdahl, *Common Man*, 1.
6. Bukdahl, *Common Man*, 1.

"belongs to the same organism as yourself you will become an Individualist" in a sense that is destructive to yourself.[7]

But despite Kierkegaard's criticism of Hegelian thought, primarily based on its being too abstract for guidance in the reality of daily living, Hegel nonetheless was responsible for shaping Kierkegaard's philosophy. John Niemeyer Findlay, the noted twentieth century professor of Western philosophy, tells us in his introduction to his commentary and review of Hegel's philosophy:

> Hegel has also had an immense, left-handed influence on thought through the reaction he inspired in the willfully narrow, passionately perverse, religious soul of the mid-century Dane Kierkegaard, whose views, despite the condemnation of Hegel, might have come straight from one of Hegel's own phenomenological studies, and whose works, like the works of those he has influenced, are soaked in an Hegelian method and spirit.[8]

The accuracy of Findlay's observation soon becomes apparent when one begins the digestion of Kierkegaard. The opening lines of Kierkegaard's *The Sickness unto Death* at once points to this Hegelian influence. *The Sickness unto Death* was published in 1849, six years before Kierkegaard's premature death. This work therefore represents the thought of a mature Kierkegaard. The volume was published under the pseudonym ANTI-CLIMACUS with Kierkegaard listed as the editor. In the work's first paragraph, Kierkegaard stated, "A human being is a synthesis of the infinite and the finite, of the temporal and the eternal, of freedom and necessity."[9]

The Deadly Error in Kierkegaard's "The Sickness unto Death"

Kierkegaard's *The Sickness unto Death* is one of his most influential works, and it is a particularly valuable work in helping one understand the basis of his Existentialism. So, we will use that work as a point of analysis to show how Kierkegaard was responsible for introducing into Western thinking the ideas that serve as the basis of existentialistic thinking. It is important to note that Existentialism is not compatible with a biblical worldview, and this

---

7. Lewis, *Mere Christianity*, 159.

8. Findlay, *Hegel: A Re-examination*, 18.

9. Kierkegaard, *Sickness*, 43.

becomes particularly clear when one comes to grip with the Existentialism that grew out of Kierkegaard's writing. In other words, when Existentialism is taken to its inevitable conclusion, it will always be found to be incompatible with a biblical worldview primarily because of the contrast that revolves around the way the two systems of thought view human nature.

Kierkegaard begins with a definition of despair which is contradictory. As the reader will note, Kierkegaard's definition of despair revolves around the self. Indeed, the entire phenomenon of Existentialism lies in the concept of self-existence. Kierkegaard writes, "Despair is a sickness of the spirit, of the self, and so can have three forms: being unconscious in despair of having a self (inauthentic despair), not wanting in despair to be oneself, and want in despair to be oneself."[10] It is in the latter two points, of course, wherein the clear contradiction lies. The plain discrepancy is resolved by realizing that Kierkegaard is speaking of two "selves." The first of the two is what he refers to as the "true self," i.e., the self that God sees; and the second is a self which belongs solely to self, with no consideration of God. And it is in this distinction where Kierkegaard's thought becomes theologically problematic.

But before we go ahead in our analysis of Kierkegaard's existentialistic concept of self and despair, let us review what we have said about the nature of Existentialism. We need to remind ourselves that Existentialism represents a philosophy which is often referred to with little understanding of what it implies. As before stated, that it is a form of Humanism is apparent by the idea that Existentialism is "carried by the thesis of the existing individual who strives for identity and meaning solely in and through his own terms"[11] This is the aspect of Existentialism that is congruous with Enlightenment Humanism, in that the humanist views all his values as coming primarily from the origin of his own person, or of his own existence. But as we first discussed in chapter 1, the area where Existentialism differs from the Humanism which evolved from the Enlightenment is in the idea of essence vs. existence. This concept will be further expanded upon when we consider Sartre, the Postmodern French existentialist who first defined Existentialism in these terms. As the Sahakians expressed it:

> Existentialists accept the conclusion that "existence precedes essence," and some go even further and affirm that essence does not exist, that only existence has reality. All Existentialists emphasize the person as subject. The subject exists, and for some he alone

10. Kierkegaard, *Sickness*, 43.
11. Barnes, *Existentialism*, v.

45

exists; that is to say, if any essence whatever exists, it is the individual subject state of existence.[12]

In other words, for the existentialist, the idea of human nature is not as one finds it to be in the Humanism derived from the Enlightenment. In classical Humanism, the idea of human personality (i.e., human nature), as shaped by the union of the intellect, emotion, and volition, is foreign to the existentialist because existence precedes essence. In Existentialism, as with the Humanism that originated in the Greek philosophy of Socrates, Plato and Aristotle, and further developed into the Humanism of the Enlightenment, man comes into the world as a blank slate with no predisposition to any particular choice.[13] He has no particular nature, but his personality (his nature) becomes formed as he begins the process of understanding reality through the functioning of the intellect and the decision-making process through the functioning of volition. As does the classical humanist, the existentialist emphasizes the freedom of the individual, but because the existentialist believes that freedom is *absolute*, man becomes *entirely* responsible for the whole of his being, simply through the process of the choices which come about necessarily, merely because of his existence.

And so, it is from the same presupposition of which Enlightenment Humanism is based upon, i.e., that one can achieve meaning and purpose through one's own self, that Kierkegaard's Existentialism is derived. Kierkegaard regarded salvation as that which is found within the desire for the true-self. Kierkegaard did not properly understand that the true-self in every human being since Adam's fall put every self under the condemnation of God. The self that every human being brings into the world is under God's wrath and, therefore, has no *ultimate* value in its unredeemed state. It is for this reason that all unredeemed "selves," will suffer eternal destruction.[14] There is no ultimate value in anyone's natural self because everyone comes into the world in rebellion against his Creator, and it is for this very reason that Jesus said, "If any man will come after me, let him deny himself, and take up his cross, and follow me. For whosoever shall save his life shall lose

12. Sahakian, *Great Philosophers*, 167.

13. Carter, *Western Humanism*, 15–19.

14. In his book, *The Fire that Consumes*, Edward Fudge argued for a non-traditional interpretation of "eternal destruction." (2 Thes 1:9.) Fudge believes that all unredeemed souls will ultimately be annihilated. However, the very words of Jesus would seem to indicate the traditional view of non-ending punishment is a more likely reality. In Matt 25:45 Jesus contrasts eternal "punishment" with eternal "life." Jesus would have used the word "death" instead of "punishment" if Fudge's interpretation was the correct one.

it; and whosoever will lose his life for my sake shall find it."[15] No one finds life, or ultimate reality, who does not first desire to lose his natural self or, to put it into biblical terms, does not understand his need to be "born again."[16]

Kierkegaard taught that there was despair in both wanting to be oneself, i.e., the self which belongs to oneself, and not wanting to be oneself, the true-self. No doubt, Kierkegaard was highly intelligent, but his understanding of the self was profoundly flawed. While Kierkegaard's understanding of despair has an element of truth, human despair lies primarily in not seeing one's self as God sees him or her, i.e., as one condemned because of one's sin nature which is sure to produce the sin that will condemn him or her. The despair of man is reflected in the attitude which gave rise to *The Beatles* song that features the phrase, "Nothing's Going to Change my World." (The song plays in the background as I write these words while sipping my coffee at the local cafe.) Kierkegaard did not understand that the man in unconscious despair is the one who sees himself as whole but is anything but whole. He is the one who is abiding within the self-satisfaction of his natural self, the self that God sees, but disapproves of. Kierkegaard wrote:

> In the main . . . despair must be considered under the aspect of consciousness; it is whether or not despair is conscious that qualitatively distinguishes one form of despair from another. Granted, when raised to the level of a concept all despair is conscious, but it does not follow that the person who is in despair, the one who according to the concept may be said to despair, is himself conscious of it. Thus, consciousness is the decisive factor. In general, what is decisive regarding the self is self-consciousness. The more consciousness, the more will; the more will, the more self. Someone who has no will at all is no self. But the more will he has, the more self-consciousness he has too.[17]

But it is the one who is in unconscious despair—the one who is satisfied in his separation from God—that has the greater self-will. It is only when one begins to understand the destruction that comes about by one's natural self-will, that one can become conscious of his despair and, thus, is enabled to turn to Christ for the remedy of that despair.

We see an excellent example of unconscious despair in the 9th chapter of John's gospel where the apostle writes of Jesus restoring the sight of an

15. Matt 6:24.
16. John 3: 3–7.
17. Kierkegaard, *Sickness*, 59.

unnamed handicapped man who had been blind from birth. The apostle John tells us that, at first, the Pharisees doubted that he had indeed been born blind, thinking that Jesus was performing some sort of fraud. After the healed man proved to the Pharisees that he had indeed been born blind, the Pharisees, instead of accepting this as evidence to the authenticity of Christ, excommunicated the redeemed man from their fellowship. We pick up the story at verse 35.

> Jesus heard that they had put him (the former blind man) out (i.e., excommunicated him) and finding him, He said, "Do you believe in the Son of Man?" He answered, "Who is He, Lord, that I may believe in Him?" Jesus said to him, "You have both seen Him, and He is the one who is talking with you." And he said, "Lord, I believe." And he worshiped Him. And Jesus said, "For judgment I came into this world, so that those who do not see may see, and that those who see may become blind." Those of the Pharisees who were with Him heard these things and said to Him, "We are not blind too, are we?" Jesus said to them, "If you were blind, you would have no sin; but since you say, 'We see,' your sin remains."[18]

What an insightful, but stinging, reply from Jesus! Jesus was here proclaiming the despair of their sin, a despair of which they had no consciousness. The source of all despair is in the knowledge of the imputation of sin, the result of which ends in the death of the soul. The one to whom sin has been imputed will be conscious of his despair when he realizes that imputation and the destruction of which that imputation implies. The source of the unconscious despair of the Pharisees was in their refusal to see their true selves, selves which were thoroughly under the wrath of God. Of course, such a blunt, truth-filled response only helped to seal the guarantee of Jesus's execution which was soon to follow.

Recall that Kierkegaard's definition of despair included three forms, one unconscious and the other two, conscious. There is no doubt that the Pharisees of this episode just referred to were unconscious of their despair. The Pharisees believed that their God viewed them with approval, as, of course, they viewed themselves. In other words, the Pharisees were in unconscious despair because they did not see themselves as God saw them. Kierkegaard acknowledges unconscious despair, but he identifies its cause as "ignorance of having a self and an eternal self." But contrary to what Kierkegaard here teaches, the Pharisees were in despair because self had

18. John 9:35–41.

become fully realized. The full realization of self is what caused their concept of reality to be formed entirely from the perspective of themselves. The natural man, i.e., the condemned man, cannot accept Christ because he has allowed himself, i.e., his true self, to rule his being. The natural true self is in rebellion against God. The Pharisees of this episode were controlled by their natural selves. Kierkegaard has simply purveyed a faulty knowledge of self, and this is what lies at the root of his Existentialism. Kierkegaard exalted the natural self, the self that God condemns. This wrong view of self carries over into one of the two forms of despair which Kierkegaard regards as conscious despair, i.e., the two forms that are contradictory, "not wanting in despair to be oneself, and want in despair to be oneself." Kierkegaard writes in his section entitled, "In despair not wanting to be oneself." The despair of weakness:

> This form of despair is: in despair not wanting to be oneself; or on an even lower level: not wanting in despair to be a self; or lowest of all: wanting in despair to be someone else, wanting a new self. Immediacy really has no self; it doesn't know itself and so cannot recognize itself either, and therefore usually it ends in fantasy. When immediacy despairs, it has not even enough self to wish or dream that it had become what it has not become. The immediate person helps himself in another way: he wishes he were someone else. One may readily convince oneself of this by observing immediate persons: in the moment of despair no wish comes more naturally to them than that they were or could become someone else.[19]

Again, it is here clear that Kierkegaard does not see that genuine conversion is only possible when one understands that it is his natural self which condemns him. It is a conversion from the natural self to a new self that saves one from condemnation. If one never sees his natural self as that which condemns him, and from that understanding wishes for a new self, then that one will never know the God of Scripture. Anyone who is to come to a true knowledge of the God of Scripture will indeed desire a new self. God will never accept any person who insists on clinging to his or her natural self.

So, in the work of Kierkegaard is established the idea that the basis for the only reality that matters is an experiential one, i.e., one that is found solely within the experience of the natural self. As stated by Barnes, the existentialist "cares only for the specific suffering person—himself, a person

---

19. Kierkegaard, *Sickness*, 83.

never free from passion and suffering."[20] And it is this outlook, as in classical Humanism, that Existentialism derives its faulty views of human freedom. For the existentialist, freedom is absolute, and thus, "the meaning of his life is to be derived from a continual engagement in a series of choices and acts," i.e., one's meaning is found solely in one's self.[21] Biblical Christianity, however, teaches that genuine meaning is found outside of one's self, in the person of Jesus Christ. Therefore, contrary to what Existentialism teaches, the moral freedom of man is not absolute freedom. Man's natural existence before God is one of condemnation. Thus, essence comes before existence. Man is only free to act according to his nature, and that nature is at enmity with God. Human moral freedom only exists as one responds correctly to God's revelation, both natural and special. The Scripture states that man "must believe that God is" (i.e., that He indeed exists, evidenced by natural revelation through the revelation of nature to include the conscience) "and that He is a rewarder of them that diligently seek Him" (i.e., one that seeks Him through the special revelation of Scripture.)[22] No one has freedom to respond to God's special revelation who has not first responded properly to His natural revelation. Man is naturally opposed to God. He is not free to be reconciled to God on his own terms. Man, desires life on his own terms but he has no freedom, as a created being, to choose life on his own terms. As I emphasized in my earlier book, man must respond to God's Word if he is to lay hold of the purpose, meaning, contentment, and peace of mind that he looks for. That contentment is found only in God's gift of grace which results in unmerited eternal life. The Christian Existentialism of Kierkegaard, the secular Existentialism of Sartre, and the quasi-secular Existentialism of Jaspers, the latter two of which we will review in the next two chapters, all put existence before essence, and thus, for the existentialist "subjectivity is always the point at which any man starts."[23]

To sum up the existential philosophy of Kierkegaard, Cochrane—many years prior to this writing—wisely framed a poignant conclusion that should help the reader understand why, for the Christian, Kierkegaard must be approached with caution. Cochrane wrote:

> In so far as I look to myself, I shall never escape an aesthetic or ethical mode of existence. I must look exclusively to Christ. This

20. Barnes, *Existentialism*, 53.
21. Barnes, *Existentialism*, 54.
22. Heb 11:6.
23. Barnes, *Existentialism*, 54.

requires not subjectivity, but the strictest objectivity. Objectivity does not necessarily mean neutrality and disinterestedness. Objectivity is the attitude in which one sees oneself changed in and by the Object—namely, Jesus Christ. In Christ we have become Christians—his members —and by the Holy Spirit we know it. True subjectivity, true existentialism, the event in which I am a person, is in the Subject Jesus Christ. So far as my subjectivity is concerned, I am one of those builders who rejected the stone. But the stone which we builders rejected has nevertheless become the chief cornerstone, the chief cornerstone of those who believe and obey. This is marvelous in our eyes. That we despair of ourselves, that we choose God, that we believe and obey, that we shall be able to understand only as a miracle wrought upon us in Christ. Man's opposition to God is immeasurably greater than . . . Kierkegaard saw. The dichotomy between pure being and existence, eternity, and time—to revert to the language of Kierkegaard's implicit ontology—is far more irreconcilable than he imagined. Otherwise, he would have given prominence to the fact that it is breached and overcome only in Christ, rather than teaching that purity of heart is to will one thing. Purity of heart is indeed to will one thing. But who is pure of heart save Christ and those for whom he willed one thing?[24]

24. Cochrane, *Existentialists and God,* 46.

4

The Secular Existentialism of Sartre

Now we come to that Postmodern Secular Existentialism which is characterized by a total denial of the supernatural. It is well characterized in the life and work of Jean-Paul Sartre. The French Sartre was born in Paris in 1905 and died there in 1978. His father was a naval officer who passed when Jean-Paul was only 2 years of age. Subsequently, Sartre was raised by his mother and his maternal grandfather in Meuden, France, a suburb of Paris. Sartre was attracted to philosophy at an early age. It is believed that Bergson's *Time and Free Will* was the stimulating impetus for the philosophical direction that would consume the rest of his life. Indeed, his philosophical education was wide in scope, as he earned a doctorate in philosophy from *E'cole Normole Supereium*, the prestigious Paris University famous for its academic exclusivity.

Certainly, all Christians would agree that *any* atheistic mindset should be characterized as humanistic in the negative sense which I have defined it. The atheistic mindset found in Postmodern Existentialism is even darker from a moral perspective than is the Secular Modern Humanism which preceded it. In the Postmodern Existentialism of Sartre all determination of what is real, of necessity, becomes totally centered in a falsely perceived sovereignty of human volition. It is in Postmodern Secular Existentialism where the rejection of any claim to absolute moral knowledge becomes a reality. While atheistic Enlightenment humanists reject supernatural reality because of misconceptions regarding the authority of science—which is based in the authority of reason—atheistic existentialists not only reject the supernatural but they will even reject the authority of reason when any goal they wish to pursue is in anyway impeded. But as we proceed with our examination of Sartre's Postmodern Secular Existentialism, we should remember that the Postmodern Non-Secular Humanism of Jaspers, examined in the next chapter, is negatively affecting contemporary Western culture to even a greater degree than does the Secular Existentialism we are here considering.

The Decline of "Enlightenment" Ideology

Because of the phenomenal successes of science in Modern Western culture, in the minds of many Westerners it once appeared that science might pave a path to an unprecedented utopia. Although Modern Humanism initially had deistic leanings it began to drift in the direction of atheism as people began to believe that human intellect could, and would, solve the many problems of human existence. But because the concept of a transcendent God was perceived to be outside the realm of empirical knowledge, and the basis for belief in the existence of God was not subject to the laboratory proof of science—which Enlightenment philosophy was then demanding for the establishment of confirmed fact—it became popular to believe that the idea of a transcendent God was an invention of wishful thinking and imagination. As a result, the atheism of the Modern era grew rapidly, particularly in the institutions of education, government, and technology, where those scientific advancements were being realized. But the optimism which science had originally generated began to fade as the midpoint of the twentieth century drew near with the ending of the bloody second world war. It soon became clear that science could not, and therefore would not, supply a means to relieve the disillusionment that the two major worldwide wars had generated. Those two wars had seen the slaughter of millions of lives, and Westerners became convinced that science would not live up to its many implied promises. It certainly became clear that the discoveries of science would never bring peace to an exceedingly troubled world. In fact, the advancement of scientific knowledge had produced the means to annihilate the entire population of the world with the pull of a few levers and/or the push of a few buttons.[1]

---

1. It is true, with atomic weapons in the possession of nations dedicated to the preservation of truth, justice and righteousness, one might argue that science could have been used to promote ultimate good. However, it is particularly ironic that in our Postmodern world, the Western nations who have the power of nuclear weapons at their command

It should then come as no surprise that Modern Humanism is slowly being replaced with the Existentialism of Postmodern Humanism. The fact that Enlightenment Humanism is losing influence does not mean that atheism in contemporary Western culture is declining, but it does mean that the basis for denying the existence of God is being based more in human volition and less so on the conclusions of human intellect. Enlightenment atheism which still has strong influence in the academy, especially in the science departments of the major universities of Western culture, is now being replaced by the atheism that is seen in the existentialistic worldview of which we are now considering, i.e., the Existentialism of Sartre. To help understand the Existentialism of Sartre, we must revisit in greater depth some aspects of that transition from the Humanism of the Modern era to that of the Postmodern era which we dealt with in chapter 2.

There can be little doubt that the realization of the impotency of science to solve the most pressing problems of human existence, is contributing to the decline of Modern Secular Humanism. As science loses influence, the significance of Nietzsche's "will to power" increases. The *major* contributing factor in the declining power of science—mainly because of its declaration of facts without proper scientific authority—is in the onset, and continuing influence, of Existentialism. It is important to remember that the Humanism coming directly out of the Enlightenment was not a Secular Humanism. Many of those early Enlightenment humanistic philosophers acknowledged God's existence, even though an understanding of the God of Scripture was remarkably absent. I discussed two of those early Enlightenment humanists in my earlier work, namely Voltaire and Immanuel Kant, who both, undeniably, held to a belief in the existence of God. Although Enlightenment Humanism culminates in atheism, Modern Secular Humanism retains the imprint of Kant's philosophy. Kant was successful at planting a seed in Non-Secular Modern humanistic thought, which carried over into Modern Secular Humanism. Kant acknowledged the natural functioning of human conscience as a guide to proper human behavior. With Kant's teaching of his "categorical imperative," which he defined as "*I am never to act otherwise than so that I could also will that my maxim should become a universal law,*" he instilled into Modern Secular

---

are actively promoting immoral lifestyles while they suppress nations which, at least, still have laws attempting to outlaw those same sexual perversions, from obtaining that same nuclear power. I am aware that the ideology that figures into this argument is not exactly straight forward, because the issue of evil vs. good is exceedingly more complex than simply the issue of sexual perversion. Nonetheless the irony remains.

Humanism the basis for a morality that yet retains the imprint of the God of Scripture. With his categorical imperative, which was recognized by Modern humanists as compatible with reason, Kant legitimized the natural role of human conscience that is spoken of in Scripture, and is compatible with those teachings of Jesus sometimes referred to as the golden rule.[2]

This brings us to Frederick Nietzsche who saw in Kant's philosophy a major conflict with his own. Nietzsche despised Kant's categorical imperative. Nietzsche was most influential in changing the course of Western Humanism from its Modern orientation, which is based in the authority of reason, to one of Postmodernism, which is based in the authority of human volition. Although Nietzsche was raised Christian, he became its bitter enemy, and he sought with great enthusiasm to destroy all Christian influence in Western culture. Nietzsche, however, was not a scientist. He was a pure philosopher whose primary philosophical interest was in debunking Christian morality. In the few short years of his productive academic life, Nietzsche was successful in turning Western philosophy away from its primary focus on the function of reason, which had been established by Plato and Aristotle, to a focus on the superiority of human volition, which became known and accepted in Western culture as his "will to power." When Nietzsche realized that Kant's philosophy had introduced into modern Western philosophy a place for the function of human conscience, his attack on Kant was relentless. In Nietzsche's own words and recorded in my prior book:

> A word against Kant as *moralist*. A virtue has to be *our* invention, *our* most personal defense and necessity: in any other sense it is merely a danger. What does not condition our life *harms* it: a virtue merely from a feeling of respect for the concept "virtue", as Kant desired it, is harmful. "Virtue", "duty", "good in itself", impersonal and universal—phantoms . . . The profoundest laws of preservation and growth demand the reverse of this: that each one of us should devise *his own* virtue, *his own* categorical imperative. A people perishes if it mistakes its *own* duty for the concept of duty in general. Nothing works more profound ruin than any "impersonal" duty, any sacrifice to the Moloch of abstraction.—Kant's categorical imperative should have been felt as *mortally dangerous*! . . . The theologian instinct alone took it under its protection.[3]

2. Rom 2:15, Matt 7:12, Luke 6:31.
3. Carter, *Western Humanism*, 156–57.

Thus, we see Nietzsche to have been a champion of the moral relativity established by the ancient Greek Sophists that Plato and Aristotle had sought to correct. Furthermore, here lies the distinguishing difference between Modern Secular and Postmodern Secular Humanism. In the Secular Humanism stemming from the Enlightenment, a place is still reserved for a natural moral guidance system found in the functioning of human conscience. In the Secular Humanism of Postmodern Existentialism is observed a philosophy that legitimizes the throw off of any moral consideration if the mind sees it helpful to immediate existence. Therefore, as we momentarily examine the thinking of Sartre, this characterizing difference will become especially clear.

It should then be clear why Nietzsche attacked Kant at this point. All human beings, unlike all other living creatures, have that natural moral guide called the conscience which gives a natural sense of right vs. wrong. When the Creator, who placed that conscience within us all, is either denied or ignored the conscience can easily cease to function as intended. Furthermore, we know from Scripture that even though belief in the existence of God might be maintained, the natural conscience can still easily become deadened. When that happens, every person decides for themselves their own standard of behavior, i.e., they do what is "right in their own eyes."[4]

And this, of course, is why Nietzsche attacked Kant's philosophy. Nietzsche taught that each person must set up their own morality. The seared conscience then becomes a distinguishing characteristic of the Postmodern humanist, both Secular and Non-Secular, because the God of Scripture is not properly acknowledged. For example, many contemporary Postmodern humanists, both Secular and Non-Secular, are trying to justify the practice of homosexuality, and deny it as moral failure, by arguing that those practices were once accepted in ancient Greece as legitimate lifestyles. While it might be difficult to prove, an argument can certainly be made, especially based upon Plato's *Symposium,* that Socrates had pederast tendencies and, if this was the case, it is certainly possible that the charges brought against him for "corrupting the youth of Athens" may have had something to do with those tendencies. It is difficult to imagine, in any system of justice, how the traditional reason given for the imposition of Socrates's death sentence could be justified or even considered to be a reasonable sentence. One must remember that Plato proposed that law should be instituted against homosexuality.[5]

---

4. Deut 12:8, Judg 17:6, Judg 21:25, Prob 30:12, Isa 5:21.
5. Plato, *Laws VIII,* 738.

Postmodern Existentialism has slowed down the trend toward the atheistic worldview to which Enlightenment Humanism once had given significant impetus. In other words, it is safe to say that with the realization of the limitations of science and the realization that the existence of a creator is more rational than is the belief that the universe simply appeared out of nothing through the processes of random chance and natural selection, the influence of Modern atheism in contemporary Western culture is decreasing in influence. But, again, this is not to say that atheism itself is on the wane in Western culture, but that the basis of that atheism is changing from reason to volition. Because of the absurdity of believing that all reality came into being by pure accident, the bulk of Westerners, to include a wide range of education levels, are refusing to believe such irrational nonsense. Most people in Western culture will still submit to the idea that something outside of time and space must have some bearing in the ultimate reality of existence. Karl Jaspers, the existentialist whom we will discuss in the next chapter is a primary example of one who was highly educated, but certainly one who would have never subscribed to a doctrine of atheism. The natural conscience bears witness to a transcendent intelligence, and most people, both those who are highly educated and those who are minimally educated, wisely choose not to go against that aspect of conscience. But before we examine that highly influential Non-Secular Existentialism, as exemplified in the work of Jaspers, we first will look at the thinking of Sartre, who indeed chose to go against the conscience that normally works to convince most people that there exists, at least, some sort of a spiritual reality which is transcendent to the universe.

Sartre and Kierkegaard

Before considering a quintessential defining lecture on Sartre's view of Existentialism, we need to put that Existentialism into perspective with the Existentialism of Kierkegaard. Some readers might perceive that the Non-Secular Existentialism of Kierkegaard has no real correspondence to the secular Existentialism of Sartre, due to the gulf that separates the mind of the atheist from the one who acquiesces to the existence of the Christian God as did Kierkegaard. But the gulf that separates a humanistic worldview from a biblical worldview involves much more than a difference in the belief of the existence of God. When one holds to a belief in the existence of a supreme being, outside of a faith that is congruous with the God and faith of Abraham, Isaac, and Jacob, his position is usually little distinguished from the one who claims that an objective knowledge of God's existence is impossible. Unless a perceived knowledge of God is based on a faith which is compatible with the complete revelation of Scripture, it can never be a genuine knowledge of God. In the biblical letter written to the Hebrews, the author makes plain that a biblical faith is evidenced based, meaning, of course, that biblical faith is completely compatible with reason, and this fact is still true whether or not that truth is acknowledged by humanistic scholars.[6]

The existentialist, be he a Secular or Non-Secular existentialist, cannot submit to an epistemology that is based in objective rational thought as it concerns both the nature of man and God. Kierkegaard and Sartre both viewed the nature of man as subjective. Human nature in the eyes of both Kierkegaard and Sartre was based solely in man's existential nature and, as such, was viewed entirely subjective to that existence. Therefore, in Existentialism there is no acknowledgment of an objective knowledge of human nature. As such, Postmodern culture has become dominated by the idea that there is no objective truth as it regards nature, be it the nature of man or even the nature of his environment. This viewpoint was the same thinking that dominated that of the ancient the Greek Sophists. Postmodern atheists, who desire that their atheism take on the appearance of that atheism that was borne from Enlightenment advancement, often take on the agnostic label, because in so doing, it keeps them within what they perceive to be a position that satisfies, if only minimally, the necessity of maintaining a rational epistemology which is necessitated by the classical humanistic system emanating from the Enlightenment. However, it is objective moral knowledge with respect to the nature of both God and man that primarily makes the existential worldview a faulty view of reality. The writings of C.S. Lewis allowed me to realize that objective moral knowledge was only possible if there was an objective supernatural reality which, of necessity is responsible for that objective morality. Kierkegaard is primarily responsible for the concept which views the truth of the nature of man as subjective. It is this concept that puts the Existentialism of Kierkegaard in-line with the Existentialism of both Nietzsche and Sartre. Furthermore, Kierkegaard's thinking was thoroughly compatible with the concept that "existence precedes essence," and it is important to remember that this quintessential saying of Existentialism was first explicitly expressed by Sartre. Therefore, while I do not believe that we can, or should, question the genuineness of

6. Heb 11:1.

Kierkegaard's faith, we should certainly proclaim that his existential view of human nature is philosophically incompatible with the truth of Scripture.

Sartre's Defining Lecture

I intend to keep the treatment of Sartre brief here because the Non-Secular Existentialism in the vein of Karl Jaspers's thinking is more challenging to understand in the context of Postmodern Existentialism. Therefore, I will limit the treatment of Sartre's atheism to a famous lecture he gave when Existentialism was first gaining its noteworthy following. However, I want to present the significant thoughts from that important lecture using Sartre's own words. As I have maintained throughout my writing on Western Humanism, for one to thoroughly understand the important historical figures of any philosophical system one must know what the originating philosophers believed, and the best way to gain that knowledge is to read the words they wrote, and not rely solely on someone else's interpretation of their words. The lecture that we will consider here was entitled *Existentialism and Humanism.* It now appears in book form, and it is still to this day one of Sartre's most widely read works.[7] Sartre delivered it to a public audience at *Club Maintenant* in Paris in October of 1945. From the title alone it is obvious that its content is particularly important to the subject of which we are here considering. Sartre here responded to the Enlightenment humanists who were criticizing the philosophy of Existentialism.

In this lecture Sartre attempted to show that Existentialism was a superior Humanism to the Enlightenment Humanism that had become prevalent during the Modern era. Sartre began his address defending Existentialism against those who viewed it as a philosophy which forces an existence in the "quietism of despair." Or to put the same sentiment into the vernacular, classical humanists were faulting existentialistic Humanism for its pessimistic worldview. In response to this charge, Sartre was quick to point out that very few people who criticize the existentialist philosophy understand what the system implies. Sartre wanted to stress the fact that Existentialism was a humanistic philosophy. Of course, Sartre was identifying the term "Humanism" with that positive connotation that is always used by Secular Humanists to convey a message of hope. But the term Humanism is better identified with the definition as I have presented it throughout

---

7. Warburton, "A student's guide to Jean-Paul Sartre's Existentialism and Humanism.", 6.

my writing. Humanism is that system of thought that is responsible for the decline of morality in Western culture, because it implies that all morality originates entirely from human sovereignty, and thus the biblical condemnation of those who do "right in their own eyes"[8] becomes validated. In other words, Sartre was teaching that this new movement called Existentialism—which would soon become highly influential in Postmodern Western culture—was a philosophy which was building on the philosophy of classical Enlightenment Humanism. Thus, under the influence of atheistic Existentialism, movement to the moral decay that proceeds with the decay of the Christian worldview continues its progress.

Sartre sought to clarify what the concept of "existence before essence" means, and he was direct in defining for his audience what is meant by that principle: He thus stated briefly:

> We mean that man first of all exists, encounters himself, surges up in the world and defines himself afterwards. If man as the existentialist sees him is not definable, it is because to begin with he is nothing. He will not be anything until later, and then he will be what he makes of himself . . . Thus, the first effect of existence is it puts every man in possession of himself as he is, and places the entire responsibly for his existence squarely upon his own shoulder.[9]

This is simply Sartre's way of saying that human beings, through their very existence are responsible for forming their own nature. Contrary to Scripture and the understanding of human nature first emphasized by Augustine in the early Christian church, the existentialist does not accept that there is in human nature a propensity to human failure because of an inherited estrangement from the God who brought all that is phenomenologically real into existence. It is for this reason that Sartre is correct in his claim that Existentialism is a humanistic philosophy. Just as Aristotle taught, Sartre claimed that man was born morally neutral with no propensity for either good or bad. It is therefore necessary for everyone to move himself to either moral wholeness or moral corruption.[10] While the intellect plays the significant role in human nature for the classical humanist, for the existentialist human volition is the primary mover for creating one's meaning and purpose.

---

8. Deut 12:8, Judg 17:6, Judg 21:25, Prob 30:12, Isa 5:21.

9. Sartre, *Existentialism and Humanism*, 28–29.

10. Carter, *Western Humanism*, 18–19.

It is interesting to note that Sartre made it a point to specifically show how the atheism of Enlightenment Humanism was distinct from the atheism of Existentialism. Sartre pointed out that when the existentialist referred to the concept of "abandonment" he was simply referring to his belief that God does not exist. The following excerpt shows particularly well how the atheism of Enlightenment Humanism differs from that of the atheism of existential Humanism:

> And when we speak of "abandonment"— a favorite word of Heidegger—we only mean to say that God does not exist, and that it is necessary to draw the consequences of his absence right to the end. The existentialist is strongly opposed to a certain type of secular moralism which seeks to suppress God at the least possible expense. Towards 1880, when the French professors endeavored to formulate a secular morality, they said something like this:— God is a useless and costly hypothesis, so we will do without it. However, if we are to have morality, a society and a law-abiding world, it is essential that certain values should be taken seriously; they must have an *a' priori* existence ascribed to them. It must be considered obligatory *a' priori* to be honest, not to lie, not to beat one's wife, to bring up children and so forth; so we are going to do a little work on this subject, which will enable us to show that these values exist all the same, inscribed in an intelligible heaven although of course there is no God. In other words—and this is, I believe, the purport of all that we in France call radicalism—nothing will be changed if God does not exist; we shall re-discover the same norms of honesty, progress and humanity, and we shall have disposed of God as an out-of-date hypothesis which will die away quietly of itself.[11]

Sartre is here essentially proclaiming that if there is no God, there is no basis for a morality that proceeds from the Judeo-Christian ethic, the ethic upon which Western culture has been built. Sartre continues, "Dostoyevsky once wrote 'If God did not exist, everything would be permitted;' and that, for existentialism, is the starting point." With anything allowed, human volition becomes supreme, because with this premise comes ultimate freedom of the will to act in any way the will sees fit to act. Sartre states this concept as follows:

> As for "despair," the meaning of this expression is extremely simple. It merely means that we limit ourselves to a reliance upon that

11. Sartre, *Existentialism and Humanism*, 32–33.

which is within our wills, or within the sum of the probabilities which render our action feasible. Whenever one wills anything, there are always these elements of probability . . . If values are uncertain, if they are still too abstract to determine the particular, concrete case under consideration, nothing remains but to trust our instincts.[12]

This is Sartre's proclamation that the criteria for all moral decision is simply to satisfy one's desire for emotional contentment by whatever means is available in any predicament. While the classical humanist seeks that same emotional contentment, he or she will often defer to reason, which should make their moral choices congruous with the morality which is based on the Judeo-Christian ethic. That ethic comes from the revelation of Scripture, and its truth will be confirmed by conscience if the conscience is not seared. It is this inherently perceived freedom, in Sartre's view, that renders the criticism of the classical humanist—who faults the existential worldview for its pessimism—as unjust. So, Sartre writes:

You have seen that it [Existentialism] cannot be regarded as a philosophy of quietism since it defines man by his action: nor as a pessimistic description of man, for no doctrine is more optimistic, the destiny of man is placed within himself. Nor is it an attempt to discourage man from action since it tells him that there is no hope except in his action and the one thing which permits him to have life is the deed. Upon this level therefore, what we are considering is an ethic of action and self-commitment.[13]

In these words of Sartre is the very essence of the Humanism that is opposed to a Christian worldview, i.e., it produces the same outcome, i.e., the sovereignty of human personality, of that which is observed in the classical Humanism which proceeded from the Enlightenment. Sartre defines the essence of man as merely his existence, which of course, is Existentialism in its purest form. He reverts to Descartes's, "I think, therefore I am," as the existentialist absolute for the definition of ultimate reality. Ultimate reality is simply found in self existence. In his own words: "Before there can be any truth whatever, then, there must be an absolute truth, and there is such a truth which is simple, easily attained and within the reach of everybody; it consists in one's immediate sense of one's self."[14]

12. Sartre, *Existentialism and Humanism*, 39, 36.
13. Sartre, *Existentialism and Humanism*, 44.
14. Sartre, *Existentialism and Humanism*, 44.

Sartre sought to justify his existentialistic Humanism against the Humanism of the Enlightenment by proclaiming that Existentialism "alone is compatible with the dignity of man." Sartre insisted that it was only existentialistic Humanism that "does not make man into an object."[15] He wrote:

> Contrary to the philosophy of Descartes, contrary to that of Kant, when we say '*I think*' we are attaining to ourselves in the presence of the other, and we are just as certain of the other as we are of ourselves. Thus, the man who discovers himself directly in the cogito also discovers all the others, and discovers them as the condition of his own existence.[16]

In Existentialism self-discovery and the resulting self-will become the only justification for living because, then, all meaning in life must necessarily be derived from self-realization, which is usually cognized as a redemptive process. But the problem with finding salvation in one's self is the fact that all selves are naturally separated from the one true ultimate reality, i.e., the God of Abraham, Isaac, and Jacob. The gulf of which I here speak is profound, and one that cannot even begin to be understood outside of the special revelation of Scripture. I repeatedly emphasized in my prior book, and have continued to bring to attention in this book, that because of Adam's disobedience human nature became so corrupt that no person living (or any who have ever lived) have any chance of achieving the redemption of self within the power of their own nature. It is eternal life that we all truly long for. But humanists want that life on their own terms, and therefore they refuse to submit their lives to Jesus, the Christ, the only means to that eternal life. No human being will ever achieve self-redemption on the merits of his or her own God-given human faculties no matter to what heights they may have reached. There is no doubt that the human intellect has achieved, and continues to achieve, many phenomenal accomplishments, but those great minds of humanity who have contributed so much to the advancement of knowledge will never be able to erase the guilt of their moral failure because of the grandeur of those accomplishments. There is not a single individual reading these words, or any who will ever read these words, who can bear witness to the *absence* of moral failure within their own existence. We all bear that guilt, and that guilt, without the appropriation of Christ's sacrifice for the sin that produced it, will eternally damn the soul.

---

15. Sartre, *Existentialism and Humanism*, 44–45.
16. Sartre, *Existentialism and Humanism*, 45.

And thus, Existentialism is, indeed, the progression of the Humanism which was birthed from Enlightenment thinking. If the truth of the one and only true God is compatible with reason and one refuses to accept that truth, the only outcome will be to reject reason when it conflicts with one's emotional and volitional dispositions. We know from Scripture that the natural man, i.e., the one outside of Christ cannot accept spiritual truth because that one will perceive it as foolishness.[17] When the un-redeemed natural person will not come to the truth of Scripture, the natural progression will be to turn to a philosophy of Existentialism. With this brief introduction into the atheism of Existentialism which denies the existence of a supernatural ultimate reality, we will now turn to that Existentialism that acknowledges the reality of a supreme being, but is one that yet leads humanity down that same path of despair as does atheistic Humanism. Belief in God's existence is insufficient for a saving trust which acknowledges Jesus as truth and as the only way to everlasting life.

17. 1 Cor 2:14.

5

The Non-Secular Existentialism of Jaspers

KARL T. JASPERS WAS born at Oldenburg, Germany in 1883 and died in Switzerland in 1969. His education was extremely broad, as he first studied law, and then medicine, before finally turning to philosophy. His philosophy was nonsectarian but it was not atheistic. Thus, in line with the definitions presented in the *Introduction* to this work, Jaspers's philosophy can be characterized as a Non-Secular Postmodern Humanism. His philosophy was highly influenced by Nietzsche and the Existentialism of Kierkegaard, and it is in Jaspers's work where we see the bridge from the Existentialism of Kierkegaard to the Existentialism which is particularly representative of the contemporary Non-Secular Postmodern humanistic worldview. As stated by Thilly and Wood:

> At the hands of Jaspers, existentialism received its most lucid, articulate and methodical formulation . . . The same preoccupation with death expressed in Kierkegaard's "sickness unto death". . . is evident in Jaspers' contention that man by virtue of his very freedom and self-transcendence is doomed to ultimate shipwreck, a destiny which he will accept freely and lovingly as the fulfillment of his being.[1]

From study of Jaspers's philosophy, further insight is gained into understanding how existentialistic Humanism is distinguished from the classical Humanism which proceeded from the Enlightenment. Humanism always presupposes that human beings have a freedom that they do not, by

---

1. Thilly and Wood, *History of Philosophy*, 587–89.

nature, truly have. No person living, or any person who has ever lived, has, or has had, the freedom to solely, in their own being, escape from the bondage of the sin nature that they have inherited from the curse of Adam. Existentialists however, unlike the classical humanists whose worldviews follow from the Enlightenment, regard their "ultimate shipwreck" as unavoidable, and therefore, identify with that shipwreck as the ultimate absurdity of the human condition. Hence existentialists must use their perceived freedom to make the best choices possible to alleviate that inevitable despair as best they can. However, the alleviation of that despair is something the existentialist can never truly accomplish. In contrast, classical humanists falsely believe that they have the power within human personality, i.e., the intellect and volitional freedom, to avoid the shipwreck and steer themselves to emotional contentment. But of course, the classical humanist is likewise self-deceived since the only resolution to the ultimate shipwreck of the human soul is in the surrender of self to Jesus, the Christ.

Jaspers's Early Existentialism

Before considering three essays which represent a mature Jaspers, we will first examine an important writing where his early thoughts on what he called "Existence-philosophy" were vividly expressed. The study of Jaspers's worldview is particularly valuable in gaining an understanding of Existentialism in general, primarily because Jaspers's life spanned the era where Existentialism went from its early conception—founded in the works of Nietzsche and Kierkegaard—to the mature atheistic Existentialism of Sartre, and Jaspers was proficient in the work of all three of these philosophers. However, it was the radical atheistic Existentialism of Sartre that caused Jaspers to shy away from wanting to be identified as an existentialist, even though he was highly influenced by Nietzsche—who, by most accounts—should certainly be classified as atheistic. I wonder if Jaspers did not regard Nietzsche as a purely strict atheist in the same manner with which Sartre so dogmatically identified. Jaspers's thinking is important because his existentialistic ideas are more consistent with the thinking of the majority of those in contemporary Western culture, than are those of Sartre who was radically atheistic. The radical atheistic Existentialism of Sartre is less commonly observed in Western culture than is the Non-Secular Existentialism that is represented by Jaspers. (Much of the humanistic atheism in contemporary

Western culture yet stems from Enlightenment Humanism, but it is that Humanism which is slowly giving way to existentialistic Humanism.)

An excellent early work to begin consideration of Jaspers's Existentialism is his volume entitled, *Man in the Modern Age*. In this work, one learns of how the influences of Friedrich Nietzsche and Søren Kierkegaard were particularly important in the formation of his philosophy. Throughout the entire book Jaspers often praised the merits of both authors. The volume was first published in Germany in 1931, that time-period where the German people found themselves between the two major world wars. Interestingly, twenty years later, when WWII had ended and existentialistic worldviews were becoming dominate in Western culture, upon reviewing this same volume for reprinting, Jaspers confirmed its (then) current relevance, and left the manuscript essentially unchanged.[2] The entire thrust of Jaspers's *Man in the Modern Age* was to document the crisis that the Modern era had created in Western culture and, what he perceived, as the existentialistic solution to that crisis. The work is of importance to our subject because Jaspers sensed the tragedy that the atheistic, materialistic worldview had perpetrated on Modern man. Speaking of the perceived sovereignty of Modern man Jaspers wrote:

> Man not only exists but knows that he exists. In full awareness he studies his world and changes it to suit his purposes. He has learned how to interfere with 'natural causation,' insofar as this is merely the unconscious repetition of immutable similars. He is not merely cognizable as extant, but himself freely decides what shall exist. Man is mind, and the situation of man as man is a mental situation.[3]

Jaspers directly attributed to Enlightenment philosophy the faulty belief that the rational aspect of human personality would pave the way to human perfection. He wrote of the Enlightenment fathers:

> The epochal consciousness entered a new phase. Beginning as the mental life of a few who knew themselves to be the true representatives of their age, it was directed, first of all, towards the glamour of a well-ordered political life, and then towards human existence as such. Now were laid the foundations of the thought that, whereas hitherto life had been accepted as it was, the human reason was

2. Jaspers, *Modern Age*, 5.

3. Jaspers, *Modern Age*, 11.

competent to mold life purposively, until it should become what it ought to be.[4]

Jaspers's grasp of the devastation of Enlightenment Humanism was surprisingly vivid and accurate. He wrote, "the modern mind has become aware of the loss of the sense of a divine presence in the world . . . ."[5] Furthermore, it appears that Jaspers was aware that the Enlightenment conception of the deistic view of God had contributed to Modern man's lost condition. He wrote:

> The idea of a transcendental creator, existing before, after, and apart from the world he had fashioned out of chaos, reduced that world to the level of a mere creature. The demons known to paganism vanished from the realm of nature, and the world became a godless world . . . Advancing doubt made an end of God the Creator, there was left in being no more than the mechanical world-system recognized by the natural sciences—a world-system which would never have been so crudely denuded of spirit but for its previous degradation to the status of a creature.[6]

So then, one is sure to ask, where did Jaspers see the solution to the bankruptcy of Modern Man, that he so readily acknowledged? We get an idea of that answer as he proceeds to discuss the role of philosophy and psychology in the context of the Modern man. Jaspers writes:

> All that is left active in him is the blind will to change the conditions and to change himself. His eagerness to do so increases, for man is incapable of living without faith. In the world of unfaith there are many who still retain the possibility of faith, but these are stifled in the germ when there is not tradition and when everyone is thrust back upon himself. However, no plan and no organization can render possible that which ultimately none can achieve except by his own activities, as man realizing the full possibility of human existence.[7]

Jaspers is here declaring that lost Modern man must find his salvation in his own activities as he realizes his own transcendent existential self, i.e., his autonomous self. Furthermore, Jaspers gives us his vision for carrying out that feat. He writes:

4. Jaspers, *Modern Age*, 13.
5. Jaspers, *Modern Age*, 25.
6. Jaspers, *Modern Age*, 25.
7. Jaspers, *Modern Age*, 140.

> Man, if he is to remain man, must advance by way of conscious-
> ness . . . Crude consciousness, whereby everything is represented
> as cognizable knowledge and as obvious purpose, is to be over-
> come by philosophy through a lucid development of all the modes
> of consciousness.[8]

That Jaspers held to a philosophy where man must save himself is plainly apparent in this work. Jaspers finishes his philosophical criticism of Modern man by stating: "No longer does the revealed Deity upon whom all is dependent come first, and no longer the world that exists around us; what comes first is man, who however, cannot make terms with himself as being, but strives to transcend himself."[9] In the mind of Jaspers, a primary nega-tive result of the Modern era was the concealment of transcendence, and as a result man was forced to attain his sense of transcendence through his own being. Furthermore, Jaspers taught that if man were to "help himself" he must do so through adapting to a "philosophy of existence." In other words, he must "become" through the inherent freedom which comes sim-ply from his existential self.

As one begins to understand the mind of Jaspers it becomes clear that in place of the lost spirituality which came by way of Enlightenment Humanism, he prescribed in its place a spirituality that is identified with a transcendental, or autonomous, existential self. Although many historians of philosophy may not recognize Jaspers as a highly influential philosopher in Postmodern thought, his remedy for the spiritual demise brought on by Enlightenment philosophy has become recognizable in Postmodern cul-ture. For example, if one reviews the self-described profiles of many people today who use the internet for social interaction, one will often come across the phrase, when describing their religious orientation, "spiritual but not religious." It is a description often used to suppose the Postmodern position which goes along the line, "Well I believe that some sort of spiritual reality probably exists, maybe even one that is transcendent to the universe, but I am not really concerned about, nor do I necessarily believe, the claim that Jesus said that he was the only way to that reality."

In his book on Postmodern thought Professor Wells writes extensively about this phenomenon of spiritualism without a scripturally based genu-ine knowledge of God and correctly identifies that phenomenon as an ever-increasing Postmodern characteristic. Wells writes:

8. Jaspers, *Modern Age*, 140.
9. Jaspers, *Modern Age*, 145.

At the heart of this development is a desire to open up windows of internal perception and to experience the sacred. Since the sacred is so often conceived as being within the self, the means of access are, correspondingly, heavily intuitive and psychological. Psychology, it has become increasingly clear, has often been assuming the role which religion once had. It is, in that sense, a secular alternative which, on purely humanistic grounds, offers what religion once provided.[10]

Furthermore, in the thinking of Jaspers, one sees an attitude towards culture that has become a characteristic feature of our own contemporary Postmodern Western environment. Ironically, contemporary Existentialism, not with intent, has succeeded in binding the individual to the herd mentality, and this has translated into a situation where the individual is pressured into conforming to a view of reality, which popular culture has determined to be the politically correct one. Jaspers writes:

> Culture brings the individual, by way of his own being, into cognizance of the whole. Instead of staying fixed in one particular place, he goes out into the world, so that, though his life be cast in narrow circumstances, it is still animated by contact with the lives of all. A man can become more decisively himself in proportion to the clarity and richness of the world with which his own reality becomes unified.[11]

As is observed in humanistic trends, Jaspers sees a complete-self as one which identifies with the culture at large, a phenomenon that is so apparent in our contemporary Western culture, where it seems that there is never ending pressure to conform to the worldview that the humanistic Western media desires to portray.

Before moving on to some examples of Jaspers's later writing, let us summarize his early ideas of what he called "Existence-philosophy," which was primarily developed through his appreciation and admiration of both Nietzsche and Kierkegaard. Jaspers writes,

> Existence-philosophy is the way of thought by means of which man seeks to become himself; it makes use of expert knowledge while at the same time going beyond it. This way of thought does not cognize objects, but elucidates and makes actual the being of the thinker. Brought into a state of suspense by having transcended

10. Wells, *Earthly Pow'rs*, 116.
11. Jaspers, *Modern Age*, 103.

the cognitions of the world (as the adoption of a philosophical attitude towards the world) that fixate being, it appeals to its own freedom (as the elucidation of existence) and gains space for its own unconditional activity through conjuring up Transcendence (as metaphysics.)[12]

It is important to note that in the Existentialism of Jaspers the concept of nihilism is something which he identifies as opposed to his "Existence-philosophy." The concept of nihilism in Existentialism can make it difficult to get a grasp on the meaning of Existentialism. For example, in the philosophy of Nietzsche—a philosophy that Jaspers was in great appreciation of—the concept of nihilism is held in tension with Nietzsche's Existentialism. While Nietzsche opposed the nothingness of nihilism, he still can be identified as a supreme nihilist, in that he wanted to wipe out the fundamental values of Western culture that had come about by many years of Christian influence. In Jaspers's existentialistic thinking, the concept of "nothingness" was a condition which had been enabled by the atheism of Enlightenment Humanism, and one which he wants to avoid by his Non-Secular ideas of Existence-philosophy, as he met in his exposure to Kierkegaard.

Unfortunately, however, Jaspers rejected the only solution to that lost human condition of which he wrote. As I study Jaspers's thought, my heart aches as I see and understand the utterly lost condition of his soul, despite the degree of learning and sophistication that his writing exhibits. It is sad to witness the refusal to accept the only source for salvation that God has provided to a human race that insists on its going its own way. Jaspers's many years of study had exposed him to the gospel message of Scripture, but it is also obvious that his idea of transcendence was yet inconsistent with the God of Scripture and more in-line with the pantheistic leanings of Spinoza. Everlasting life is only found in the atonement for sin obtained through the sacrifice of Jesus Christ. The exceedingly interesting, but tragic aspect of Jaspers's thought, is the fact that while he was poignantly aware of the spiritual bankruptcy of the Modern age, he nonetheless did not understand the relevancy of Jesus Christ as the solution to that bankruptcy. As do so many people in our contemporary Western Culture, Jaspers sought to hold to a spiritual reality without acknowledging and submitting to the God of Ultimate Reality, i.e., the God of Abraham, Isaac, and Jacob.

12. Jaspers, *Modern Age*, 159.

Jaspers's Mature Existentialism

Now we turn to the thoughts of Jaspers's emanating from the post-war (WWII) years, where his ideas became more entrenched in a Humanism which seemed to drift away from his earlier emphasis on the transcendental, to that of a more practical Humanism, yet one that came from his existential philosophy. A compilation of three of his essays entitled *Existentialism and Humanism*[13] was published in the years following the war when Germany, as a defeated nation, was struggling for a meaningful survival. As one might conclude from the title, this work seeks to reinforce the fact that Existentialism, while distinguished from the Humanism proceeding from the Enlightenment, is yet characterized as a philosophy that attempts to achieve spiritual wholeness solely within human power, instead of portraying the term (Humanism) as I have presented it throughout my writing on the subject, i.e., as a philosophy that fails to acknowledge the utter separation of humanity from the one true ultimate reality, because of an inherited nature which has been passed down from the first man, Adam. We will briefly consider these essays to better understand the mature Existentialism of Jaspers and how it yet relates to the classic Western Humanism which is derived from Enlightenment thinking. The work's editor states in his introduction to the volume:

> Here lies one strong root of the persuasiveness of existentialism. Without being strictly irreligious it does address mainly those who are no longer capable of belief—or, better, of further adherence to traditional ecclesiastic or religious views . . . Existentialism does not suppose to explain the world; its aim is to explain man and to help him face the world. Both Jaspers and Heidegger are certain that the roots of existence lie in the transcendent sphere, even if the second denies its religious nature and both of them seem to dispense with a personal God.[14]

The first two of the three essays in this work of Jaspers features mini-character studies of the ancient Greek leader Solon and of the nineteenth century German poet, Goethe. In his essay entitled *Solon* is Jaspers's account of that ancient Greek statesman who lived during the turn of the sixth century BC, and to whom Plato pays tribute in his *Timaeus*. In Plato's

13. This is the exact same title that was used in Sartre's work presented in the previous chapter, so I here use the subtitle (*Three Essays*) when referring to Jaspers's work with that same title.

14. Jaspers, *Three Essays*, 10.

Timaeus, he praised Solon as "the greatest of the Seven Sages." Jaspers tells us that his intention in the essay is to "restate known facts of Solon's life and thought, in an arrangement and a characterization based on love and worship of the spirit of man."[15] With this description, Jaspers puts forth the very essence of the Humanism with which we are here concerned; all humanistic philosophy is essentially reduced to "love and worship" of the human spirit. Even though the love and worship of the human spirit has become a common-place reality in our Postmodern world, any worship of the human spirit is a misdirected worship, since only the creator of the human spirit is worthy of that worship. Solon is best known for the courage he displayed in capturing Salamis Island from the tyrant Megara. The island presented problems with free access to the port of Athens and many prior Greek leaders had attempted to conqueror it, only to meet with defeat and death. Solon justified his conquest with the belief that Salamis rightfully belonged to Athens because it had, in days gone by, been in the hands of the Athenians. Solon was subsequently hailed as a hero and became an Athenian political leader later noted for his problem-solving skills in social matters. Under Solon, slaves were freed, financial systems were reformed, and laws were established to bring about order and peace.

Jaspers hails Solon as an existential-humanistic hero because he perceived that Solon sought to right those social wrongs that will inevitably appear in all cultures. Human nature, if left unchecked by the grace of God, will always eventually produce societies with two primary economic classes. Jaspers's example was taken from history when the social conditions that existed in ancient Greece were not unlike the conditions of nineteenth century Russia, which ultimately resulted in the communistic socialism of Karl Marx. The philosophy of Marx and Engels was the result of their humanistic attempt to solve the social problems which result from those two economic extremes. The sin of greed, the sin that leads to a condition where the middle class is endangered in cultures where the influence of the God of Scripture is absent, is a sin to which every human being, outside of the grace of God, is susceptible. And in post-Christian, Postmodern America, the same trend towards those two extremes is becoming ever more apparent. The two classes of which I speak consist of one where there is an obsession to ever increasing wealth, and the other class is where there exists simply the struggle to survive. It is well known that many cultures exist throughout the world where the middle class is almost visibly absent. If you

15. Jaspers, *Three Essays*, 19.

travel in the Philippine Islands for example, you will see the combination of unimaginable poverty living along side of lavish wealth that is on par with the most advanced countries in the world. There has always been a humanistic effort to level out the extremes of these two primary economic classes of which we speak. In all contemporary cultures, a leftist faction is at work looking to find a means for redistributing wealth from the upper to the lower economic classes. It is an effort that has always been in progress and, no doubt, always will be. Because the Scriptures portray Jesus as a friend to the poor, oftentimes this leftist appeal for redistribution of wealth is framed in a Christian context. No better example of this is seen in the movement known as Liberation theology which proceeded from certain South American Roman Catholic entities in the mid twentieth century. In that movement the outreach to the disadvantaged with the gospel of Christ was replaced by an effort focused entirely on economic concerns.

An event from the life of Christ concerns this issue of economic parity and, as such, gives the Christian moral guidelines on the issues involved. Although Jesus was concerned with those of low economic status, his primary concern was with the status of one's spiritual condition. As Mark tells us in chapter 14 of his gospel, Jesus was at the house of a certain leper named Simon where a woman, who was also a guest in that same company, took a container of expensive perfume (worth about three thousand dollars in current currency) and poured it over his head. Some of those present who had seen the event became indignant at what appeared to them to be a gross waste of wealth and proceeded to rebuke the woman for her generous gesture, saying that the money should have be redistributed to the poor. We pick up Jesus's response to those who verbally chastised her in verse 6: "Let her alone; why do you bother her? She has done a good deed to Me. For you always have the poor with you, and whenever you wish you can do good to them." The push for economic equality is more of a humanistic concern, and less so a Christian one, because socialism never addresses the primary issues that lie at the ultimate reasons for the dichotomy that it is trying to address. I have made it a habit in my own personal life, when financially helping the homeless on the street, to always give witness to the saving power of Jesus Christ, because this is usually the primary need of those who are seeking financial relief in that manner.

Furthermore, this illustration by Jaspers—of Solon as an existentialistic hero—is further exemplified in the effort of Solon's will to conquer solely based on selfish desire. Here we see the transition from reason, to human volition, as exemplified in the teachings of both Nietzsche and, more subtlety, in Kierkegaard. Solon simply exerted his will in the taking of Salamis. He wanted and therefore he acted from a "will to power" in the tradition of Hitler and in Hitler's hero, Nietzsche. Solon had the power to choose and he chose according to the mere dictates of his will. In the Scriptural letter to the Thessalonians is a reference by the apostle Paul to what he calls "the mystery of lawlessness."[16] This appears to be a condition in society where law is simply dismissed in favor of a "will to power" and it appears that the disregard for law in favor of the personal desires of rulers will become increasingly important in deciding public policies as existentialistic Humanism becomes more prevalent in Western culture. Contemporary examples of this phenomenon are not difficult to document. The Attorney General of Pennsylvania once stated that she would not "defend the state's traditional marriage law in court,"[17] because of her personal beliefs of the legitimacy of homosexual marriage. And of course, the matter of illegal immigration in the United States supplies another outstanding contemporary example of this principle. When US President Trump sought simply to enforce the law in regards to illegal immigration, he was met with an unprecedented resistance by those who simply desired to have their own way about the issue.

In Jasper's essay entitled *"Our Future and Goethe"* is more fodder for better understanding how Jaspers's Existentialism is thoroughly congruent with Humanism as I have defined it throughout my writing on the subject. The opening statement of Jaspers's essay speaks to the despair that, no doubt, was prevalent in the German nation at the close of WWII. Jaspers began his essay with the following words: "A catastrophe of the West, indeed of mankind was sensed by old Goethe, more and more clearly foreseen by Niebuhr, Stendhal, Tocqueville, Burckhardt, wholly grasped by Kierkegaard and Nietzsche, and expected to lead to final salvation by Marx." The catastrophe which "old Goethe" sensed was the industrial and scientific revolution that contributed to the perceived demise of individuality that the Modern era had introduced into Western culture. Possibly Jaspers was also alluding to these philosopher's anticipation of the destructive technology which had just contributed to an unprecedented loss of life, and the fact that war technology had then advanced to even greater destructive capability with the advent of nuclear weapons. The essay was written at the close of WWII after Germany's devastating loss, and the future looked quite bleak for Germany.

16. 2 Thess 2:7.

17. Beltz, "Pastor Arrested," para. 1.

At this point in his life Jaspers was rethinking that his appreciation of Nietzsche's philosophy was worthy of further questioning. Although Jaspers was opposed to the Nazism that had resulted in Germany's ruin, Nietzsche's philosophy certainly reflected a spirit that ringed with sympathy for the conquest that Hitler had pursued. In the essay Jaspers contrasted Nietzsche and Goethe with the following words:

> Nietzsche keeps forcing negation, traverses all forms of nihilism, grapples fiercely with his tenets of the day, lives in an atmosphere of aggressiveness, despair, lovelessness, manic faith. He provokes battle. He torments us, and we let ourselves be tormented because we find him advancing us vitally toward the truth. Goethe lives by affirmation. He loves the world, life, all things, and all men. He urges conciliation and agreement. He promotes compromises. An atmosphere of benevolence and kindness pervades his every remark. This is what makes it so gratifying to reach for Goethe time and again, to invigorate our own impulses of loving study, of conciliatory affirmation, or reason and sobriety, of open-mindedness for the wealth of the world and of man-kind whenever they threat to fail us.[18]

Here the reader senses that Jaspers was urging his fellow Germans to reconsider the mental framework which had propelled them to their current condition of national humiliation. Goethe had once been a point of pride for the German people due to the worldwide acknowledgment that his literary work, particularly his *Faust*, had procured. However, the more we learn about "old Goethe" both as a person and as a philosopher, the more we realize the utter folly of looking for national redemption in the character of Germany's long-forgotten literary hero. As Strong, who had researched Goethe's life and personality with thoroughness, tells us, "Goethe was a man without conscience; he was the instrument of a merely literary emancipation, while he re-established, so far as he could, the reign of pagan self-dependence and of moral indifference."[19] It is in the philosophy and theology of Goethe, whom Jaspers obviously admired, where we can gain a better understanding for Jaspers's own theology. In Jaspers's referrals to deity, he often uses the language which is normally used in the terminology of monotheism. But from the known facts of Goethe's belief system comes

18. Jaspers, *Three Essays*, 59.
19. Strong, *Great Poets*, 282.

the understanding that he was sympathetic to the pantheism of Spinoza. Strong, speaking of the belief system of Goethe wrote:

> [Goethe] . . . would develop all sides of his nature, gain all sorts of experience, taste all the pleasures that life could give. It was a pagan culture which he set himself to attain. He was "the great heathen" of modern times, and he was not ashamed to be known as such. He hid his face from the pain and suffering of the world, as the old Greeks did. The Cross of Christ, with its vicarious love and sorrow, was repulsive to him, for it was a contrast and rebuke to his self-indulgent, self-seeking, self-exalting spirit. Goethe had in his heart turned away from the true God—the personal God, the God of holiness, the God who imposes moral law, the God who offers pardon through Christ—and he had put in his place a God of his own wishes and imagination, a nature-God, a God without personality or moral character, a God to whom evil and good are both alike, because both alike proceed from him, a God who is best served, not by self-restraint and self-sacrifice, but by the unhindered development of all our inborn instinct and powers.[20]

Notwithstanding that Goethe lived before Existentialism gained its dominance in Western culture, elements of Jaspers's "Existence philosophy" are clear in the description of Goethe's character that Strong has provided for his reader. Although atheistic worldviews in the vein of Sartre continue to have their place in Postmodern Existentialism, the Existentialism that acknowledges and even promotes a philosophy which includes a transcendental deity must also be reckoned with in Postmodern thought. However, that transcendental deity will always stand opposed to the God of Scripture.

In the final essay of the collection of Jaspers's writings that we are here considering, we witness Jaspers's specific interest in the movement from the "classical" Humanism of the Enlightenment to the Existentialistic Humanism of Postmodernism. In the essay entitled *Premises and Possibilities of a New Humanism*, Jaspers pursues three major questions in his quest for promoting a Postmodern Humanism. These are (1.) What is man? (2.) What actual conditions govern humanity now? (3.) What way of Humanism seems possible to us? Jaspers's existentialistic answer to the first of these questions is like what is observed in the philosophy of Kierkegaard. The existence of man is not seen primarily in a situation which is characterized as being separated from the God of Scripture because of a nature that is

---

20. Strong, *Great Poets*, 295.

thoroughly infested with one's desire to "go his own way."[21] Man's existence is found primarily in his freedom to "go his own way." Instead of human volition responding to intellect for guidance in living the "good life" as in the case of the classical Humanism that originated in ancient Greece, absolute freedom of will, a will not bound by the intellect, now becomes the defining characteristic of human existence. Unfortunately, Jaspers saw in human freedom, a freedom which by necessity voided the exclusive claims of Jesus when Jesus proclaimed, "I am the way, the truth and the life. No man cometh unto the Father but by me."[22] Thus, Jaspers rejected the objective knowledge that human nature is naturally corrupted because of Adam's sin. When anyone rejects this truth, their entire belief system, on human nature and its relationship to the God of Scripture, is automatically out of kilter with reality. Jaspers states: "What man is cannot be attributed to any knowledge about him. It can only be learned at the source non-objectively, beyond all that can ever be known."[23] While Jaspers was quick to acknowledge human limitations, he yet put his hope, not in the God of Scripture, the only source of sincere hope, but in a falsely perceived human freedom. When speaking of future humanity, Jaspers stated: "I go to the root of human freedom; I appeal to our will . . . If we can ascertain humanity in the encompassing framework of its potentiality, we can never quite despair of man."[24] Jaspers's Existentialism was clearly bound to a Humanism in the negative way I have defined it.

In Jaspers's address to his second question he focused on the changes that scientific advancements had brought to human consciousness. Jaspers referred to these changes as the "disintegrating consciousness of the masses." Jaspers expressed hope for this disintegrating consciousness in "hidden, human realities: powerful love, heroism and deep faith." The "deep faith" Jaspers refers to here is not the faith in the God who sent his only begotten son, the Christ, to save humanity from the certain death that sin brings. If that had been the case, we would not be discussing Jaspers's philosophy in the context of Postmodern Humanism. Jesus promised that he would return to the earth to set up a kingdom of righteousness, and all who have faith in that promise do indeed have a glorious future to look forward to. In dealing with his final question, Jaspers reminded his reader that Western

21. Isa 53:6.
22. John 14:6.
23. Jaspers, *Three Essays*, 69.
24. Jaspers, *Three Essays*, 73.

Humanism had provided humankind with a grand tradition in education, and he encouraged the continuation of that tradition. Jaspers stated that "Humanism is essentially a matter of education," and surprisingly, he even recommended that Western children should become familiarized with the "history of antiquity" to include that of the Bible.[25] Certainly, Jaspers's wishes here have been fulfilled regarding the use of the educational systems of Western culture for the furtherance of humanistic indoctrination. However, there is seldom, if ever, allotted the opportunity for any objective study of Scripture in the contemporary humanistic agenda.

With the consideration of the life and work of Karl Jaspers, it becomes apparent that just as there was observed in the Non-Secular Humanism which proceeded out of Enlightenment Humanism, a Non-Secular Humanism is poignantly present in the Humanism which now dominates Postmodern Western culture. It is important to remember that the enemy of the one true God, that evil one called Satan, is never threatened by the one who simply believes in the existence of deity. As we read in Scripture, "You believe that God is one. You do well; the demons also believe, and shudder."[26] Believing in the existence of God does not alleviate the separation from God and subsequent condemnation by God that all human beings are under. Scripture cannot be more explicit in the fact that all humans, outside of the provision of Jesus Christ, are under condemnation. The apostle John writes in his gospel:

> For God sent not his Son into the world to condemn the world; but that the world through him might be saved. He that believeth on him is not condemned: but he that believeth not is condemned already, because he hath not believed in the name of the only begotten Son of God. And this is the condemnation, that light is come into the world, and men loved darkness rather than light, because their deeds were evil.[27]

There is no doubt that the goal of Humanism is a genuine quest for a perceived good. Jaspers's writing was entirely consumed with seeking what he perceived as good for humankind. Even Karl Marx would have insisted that he was seeking good for humanity as he put forth his ideas of communism. However, the moral good that all humanists seek, be it the good coming from a belief system that denies the existence of God, or one that

25. Jaspers, *Three Essays*, 86.
26. James 2:19.
27. John 3:17–19, (KJV).

acquiesces to the obvious truth of God's existence, is a search that can never come to realization. It is so difficult for the human mind to understand that the only source of good originates not in man but in the God of Scripture. Scripture describes the goodness that emanates from human nature as an inferior good to the true good. The prophet Isaiah said it succinctly: "For all of us have become like one who is unclean/ And all our righteous deeds are like a filthy garment; And all of us wither like a leaf/And our iniquities, like the wind, take us away."[28] As the KJV translates it, the virtuous deeds which spring solely from human nature are like "filthy rags." This is a truth that all humans, myself included, simply abhor in our lost condition and, therefore, all of us are prone to reject it. Indeed, most all people do reject that truth. We all want to believe that there is inherent true good within human nature, a nature that is separated from the true good because of the sin of our first parent, Adam.

The Scripture records for us another example from the life of Jesus that so well addresses the issue of which we here speak, i.e., the human tendency to misperceive the nature of true good. This example is of such significance, that all three of the synoptic gospels give an account of the episode. I speak of the account of the rich young ruler who comes to Jesus to ask what he must do to inherit eternal life.[29] The incident demonstrates so clearly the common misconception of good. It is a misconception which has existed in human nature since the beginning of time. It was present in ancient Greece, it was present in the time of Jesus, and it yet persists to this day. This error in belief lies at the very heart of the error of the whole concept of Humanism in general. Furthermore, the incident gives witness to the infinite wisdom of Jesus, and demonstrates particularly well the actual deity of Jesus. I marvel at Jesus's response to this young, rich, and powerful man, who came to Jesus with the address of "Good Master." When he addresses Jesus with that greeting, Jesus responds with the words, "Why do you call me good? There is none good but God." Jesus was trying to show the young man that his concept of good was in error. Jesus does not deny his goodness, but the young man had no idea that he was speaking with the very God of creation. Jesus wanted to show the young man, who wrongly believed that he himself was a good man, that his idea of goodness was not

28. Isaiah 64:6.
29. Matt 19, Mark 10, Luke 18.

80

founded in truth. His idea of good was a humanistic idea of good and that misperceived concept of good is what led to his probable condemnation.[30]

Summary of Part I

In the summary of Part I of this work, I need to emphasize that a major error of Postmodern Humanism is the existentialistic belief that since the primary characteristic of human nature is simply existence, concepts of good versus bad, evil versus righteousness, right versus wrong are relative to a given existence. Therefore, in Existentialism, the individual, based upon her own personally determined worldview, needs to decide for herself what is her personal truth. In the mind of the existentialist, there are no absolutes and all truth is therefore subjective, even the matter of God's existence. In existentialistic thinking, if one needs to believe in a higher power, or in an absolute good based in a concept of deity, then that is fine for that particular person, but that standard of reality should never become a universal standard which applies to all people. There can be no absolutes on what is to be viewed as universal, and therefore each existing individual must decide from the freedom of their own being what will serve as the ultimate good for them. Furthermore, it is this thinking which has given rise to the decline of the Enlightenment ideal. Enlightenment Humanism is based in the idea that human reason is the only means for finding what is real. Because the function of human reason does indeed play a primary role in the determination of physical truth, the extraordinary discoveries of science in the last few years of history led many to believe that if a truth claim cannot be proven by the scientific method then it cannot be declared as a fact. In Enlightenment reasoning, science therefore became the ultimate standard by which to judge all truth claims. However, humanistic scientists began to make the claim that the cosmos is all there is without the scientific proof that they claim must be present to make that claim. Therefore, science has discredited itself because it has attempted to speak with authority where it has none. But to use the well-known saying, Existentialism wants to throw the baby out with the bathwater. Kierkegaard's "leap of faith" which would seem to approximate a "leap in the dark" is not a proper view of biblical faith. Faith in the God of the Scripture is far from a leap in the dark; it

---

30. Of course, I must include the word "probable" here because Scripture does not give us any information on this man's final decision, but it certainly does imply a choice which probably cost him the eternal life he was seeking.

is clearly evidence based, as we will discuss in the next chapter. True, the Enlightenment ideal that teaches that human reason is the only qualifier to all truth claims must indeed be challenged. But to trade the Humanism of the Enlightenment for the Humanism of Existentialism is not an advancement of knowledge. Humanism is still Humanism, which is a view of reality which remains contrary to the ultimate reality of Scripture, the God of Abraham, Isaac, and Jacob.

PART II

Contemporary

6

Epistemology and the "Worldview"

THE THRUST OF MY writing on Humanism has been to show it as a faulty worldview that now dominates the thought processes of the vast majority of those in Western culture. While the Modern Humanistic worldview is distinct from that of the Postmodern one, both humanistic systems of thought are based on the false premise that man has sovereignty over his own moral nature. The ultimate end of Modern Humanism is one of either atheism or agnosticism, and the ultimate end of Postmodern Humanism is an indifference to the existence of any reality outside of the immediate concerns of self-existence. Western Humanism began with the acknowledgment of a supreme being, but it has migrated to a philosophy where the one true God, the God of Scripture, no longer plays any meaningful role in the worldviews which are most prominent in Western culture. The worldview that derives from an acknowledgment and proper understanding of the authority of supernatural revelation, of course, has been challenged ever since the beginning of human existence; but it was in Western culture where that worldview, which is based in the knowledge of the one and only true God, became particularly influential and yielded the scientific knowledge from which the whole of civilization has benefited. The decline of godly influence in Western culture is particularly why the story of Humanism is one of tragedy, not unlike the tragedy seen in the bulk of the Jewish population, who once having had revealed to them the very oracles of the God of creation, likewise turned away from the revelation of their Messiah and towards beliefs which resulted in the loss of that once elevated perception of reality.

The acquisition of any worldview is closely aligned with the subject of epistemology. Epistemology is that study which has to do with understanding how one acquires knowledge or, better stated, of how one comes to an understanding of that which is real, or true. Epistemology has a direct bearing on how one's worldview is formed. For example, is the German perpetrated Holocaust of WWII a reality of history? Some people might genuinely believe that the historical account of the Holocaust is an exaggeration of Nazi atrocities, contrary to what all people who have been genuinely educated know to be true. How does one know that millions of Jews were murdered even though probably most of those reading these words were either not alive or were far removed from the locale when and where those atrocities occurred? Both viewpoints concerning the reality of the Holocaust consist of belief, even genuine belief, but both positions cannot be correct. The statement which declares that millions of Jews were murdered by the Nazi Third Reich, primarily between the years of 1941 to 1945, for no other reason than the fact that they were Jews, is either true or false; it cannot be both true and false.[1] Therefore, most often, the basis for forming any worldview which is based in truth must come down to issues of trust in authoritative sources. Since few people living today have direct, first-hand knowledge of what occurred in the concentration camps of the German Third Reich; one must gain knowledge of that subject by trusting the authority of sources who have recorded first-hand knowledge of those events.

Often not considered in epistemology is how and why worldviews, opposing what is true, even come into existence. For example, what triggers any belief that is not founded in reality? How could, or why would, anyone develop the belief that the reality of the German originated Jewish Holocaust is a falsehood? The answer to that question lies in the existential influence on Postmodern epistemology which is now, unfortunately, the reality in Postmodern thinking. The deemphasis in what is rational—or in other words—the de-emphasis of the intellect, in deference to what one wants to be true, or what one wills to be true, is the controlling factor that results in false views of reality. In other words, there are those who seriously debate that the Holocaust happened, as history has recorded it, because of biased desires regarding what they want to be true. There is no true

1. This same scenario applies to many other similar historical events which some peoples might wish had recorded histories other than those generally acknowledged in worldviews based in truth. The killing of Armenian Christians by the Turks of the Ottoman Empire, during the era of the WWI, immediately comes to mind as another outstanding example that show how worldviews can be formed which go contrary to fact.

objective examination of the facts in reaching their false conclusions. Thus, false views of reality are thereby engendered, enabled, and perpetuated.

Scientific Authority

Therefore, the subject of epistemology has an intimate connection with the subject of philosophy. Philosophy is the subject that is concerned with the love of wisdom, truth, and knowledge. Therefore, the main goal of philosophy in Western culture, ever since the Greek Presocratic philosophers, has been to come to an understanding of what constitutes a genuine concept of a reality which is, in fact, based upon truth. In the early development of Greek philosophy, the Greek Presocratic philosophers thought that an ultimate reality not apparent to the senses, i.e., a pantheistic type deity, might be responsible for the existence of all that which is perceived phenomenologically. The Sophists resisted that idea by denying any reality apart from that which is perceived by the senses. Before Plato and Aristotle, the Sophists taught that ultimate reality was unknowable, and therefore, whatever anyone might believe constitutes truth was valid for that particular perceiver. Therefore, the art of rhetoric, according to the Sophists, should be emphasized because the knowledge of what is real would then be decided by skill in debate. The arguments from reason used by Plato and Aristotle were successful for showing the Sophists their ultimate error. Thus, the epistemological course of Western philosophy was set in the authority of human reason until Nietzsche began to turn it back to a Sophistic type of thinking where the denial of absolute truth became commonplace. The Humanism that began in classical Greek philosophy—centered in the philosophies of Plato and Aristotle—which acknowledged a transcendent intelligence was driven on the assumption that by human reason one could arrive at the ultimate good and the ultimate truth of reality. It is that basic thinking which prevailed in Western philosophy up until the recent onset of Existentialism. The Enlightenment ideal, one based in the authority of reason, however eventually led to the Secular humanistic worldview that brought about the rejection of the supernatural and yielded the philosophy of naturalism. Naturalism thereafter became the dominant philosophy in Modern Western culture, primarily through the influence of Charles Darwin, and it is based in the idea that the entirety of reality is represented within the order of the natural universe. Naturalism was not however, a complete return to the worldview of the ancient Greek Sophists. The Greek Sophists denied even the possibility of obtaining absolute knowledge on the nature of the physical universe, while the philosophy of the Modern era became focused on the idea that *all* knowledge must be derived through scientific reasoning. The idea that all knowledge must come through the authority of science then became falsely established as fact within Western culture.

There can be little doubt that the Humanism of the Enlightenment rose to prominence because of the success of the scientific method. But unfortunately, Enlightenment thinking led to the false philosophy of naturalism where the idea that anything that lies outside the reality of the physical cosmos simply cannot exist. Secular Humanism, based in atheism, thus became prominent in Western culture, particularly so in Western higher education because of the false belief that the "cosmos is all there is" as Cornell's Sagan so boldly proclaimed. Because of Sagan's popularity, that declaration appealed to many humanists, both those in the Postmodern atheistic tradition of Sartre as well as those in the Modern humanistic tradition of Darwin. The atheistic mind of Modern Humanism only accepts the authority of science while the atheistic mind of Existentialism will not necessarily discriminate based on science, but they both absolutely refuse to acknowledge any absolute authority based in Holy Scripture.

But of course, this does not make the claim that there is authoritative knowledge in science a false claim, because there is certainly authoritative knowledge which is imparted by the authority of science. It is the ignorant person who claims otherwise. But the materialistic atheist has set up science as his ultimate reality, i.e., his god, and the evidence that he has done just that is quite apparent to the observant mind. If the assumption that the "cosmos is all there is," were to be proven true, then science *would indeed* become the only workable means for the determination of all truth. However, there is *absolutely no* evidence that this belief is true. Sagan unfortunately showed a particular ignorance by choosing to adamantly deny any possibility of God's existence. He thus purported a worldview that is not subject to the proof of science, the authority in which he placed his greatest trust. The statement that "the cosmos is all there is" is a philosophical conclusion, and it is not a fact that is founded in scientific knowledge. Therefore, many materialistic atheists in the Modern tradition feel the strong need to accept the *possibility* of God's existence. The agnostic position is thus an atheistic position usually taken on to keep oneself within the appearance of a rational framework. In 2008 Richard Dawkins, along with The British Humanist Association, sponsored a sign campaign in Britain where the sign read, "There probably is no god. Now stop worrying and enjoy your life." While the message of that campaign was agnostic, the essential intent of it was an atheistic one.

In his brief work, *Escape from Reason*, the popular evangelical philosopher/theologian of the latter half of the twentieth century, Francis Schaeffer, discussed the divide between "the particulars" of the lower realm and "the universals" of the upper realm in the vein of Plato's Theory of Forms. Schaeffer labeled the universals of the upper realm with what he called, "true truth" while he placed the subject of mathematics in the lower realm of particulars.[2] But it is because mathematics is indeed "true truth" that Schaeffer established a questionable compartmentalization. And of course, with this argument I am not in any way discrediting the claims of inspired Scripture where the Apostle states that in Christ are "hidden all of the treasures of wisdom and knowledge."[3] Obviously, the Creator knows the intricate details of nature in their entirety of which science has only barely begun to uncover. A drop of water as compared to all the water of the oceans of the entire world does not suffice in comparing what has become known of nature by the scientific method to that which still is unknown to man and is yet known only by the Creator. And therefore, the authority of mathematics and science will never trump the authority of Scripture. But science is indeed a legitimate means to a working knowledge of natural phenomenon primarily when it is grounded in the absoluteness of mathematics. The fact that two cubed is eight is true truth.

Lord Kelvin, the brilliant scientist of the nineteenth century, whose name honors his creation of the absolute temperature scale, made a saying popular among many scientists, when he stated that if any subject could not be described numerically then that subject could not be classified as science. And a genuine scientist should be sympathetic to this declaration. I had an undergraduate physics professor who enjoyed poking fun at the subject of organic chemistry, because there was too little mathematics involved in the subject to master it. What he did not acknowledge, however, is the fact that the four sp3 hybrid orbitals of carbon which are responsible for binding the carbon atom in its notorious tetrahedral configuration can only be described in terms of mathematics, despite the fact that the undergraduate organic chemistry student has not progressed far enough in his studies to handle the advanced mathematics of quantum chemistry necessary to

2. Schaeffer, *Escape*, 18.

3. Col 2:3.

have a working knowledge of chemical bonding at the atomic level. Furthermore, the subject of quantum mechanics relies heavily on the concept of mathematical probability, a scenario that even Einstein had problems with because of its opposition to intuition. Einstein is famous for questioning the probability underlying the science of quantum mechanics. He is well known for his statement where he declared that he did not believe that "God plays dice with the universe." But despite Einstein's objections, quantum mechanics, because of the authority of mathematics, has triumphed as a working scientific model. Quantum theory correctly describes the behavior of subatomic phenomena. Therefore, quantum theory stands because the experimental results, from which the theory's conclusions are drawn, can be repeatably demonstrated in the laboratory. How ironic that the authority of mathematics trumped even the objections of the most famous scientist of the twentieth century whose own contributions to science, namely his theories of relativity, cannot be divorced from their grounding in the authority of mathematics.

Therefore, with the unprecedented success of science, most of the established knowledge concerning the nature of the cosmos has come about because of the scientific method, i.e., the method based upon the well-known algorithm consisting of hypotheses, experiment, results, and conclusion. But it is important to understand that the scientific hypothesis is a presupposition which can only be used to probe physical reality as it exists under the conditions at the time of the presupposition. One reason that the subject of philosophy is so fascinating is because in the teachings of every world-renowned philosopher, there can be discovered an element of truth, or at least a sliver of such, no matter if the overall position of the philosopher is one of error. Even the atheistic David Hume so wisely acknowledged the problem of trying to derive knowledge based in the authority of human inductive reasoning where the uniformity of nature is presupposed. Stated Hume:

> It may, therefore, be a subject worthy of curiosity, to inquire what is the nature of that evidence which assures us of any real existence and matter of fact, beyond the present testimony of our senses, or the records of our memory."[4]

Hume taught that inductive reasoning could be imperfect when an accounting of reality was dependent upon a situation which was "beyond

---

4. Hume, *Enquiry*, 458.

the present testimony of the senses, or the records of our memory." Hume reasoned that just because the sun rises every morning, it would not necessarily be irrational if that event were, someday, not to happen. Hume writes:

> That the sun will not rise to-morrow is no less intelligible a proposition, and implies no more contradiction than the affirmation, that it will rise. We should in vain, therefore, attempt to demonstrate its falsehood. Were it demonstratively false, it would imply a contradiction, and could never be distinctly conceived by the mind.[5]

The truth that Hume was alluding to points to a serious flaw in contemporary scientific reasoning. The dating methods which describe a universe that is billions of years old are usually based on models that unreasonably assign a uniformity to nature that simply does not exist because of, if for no other reason, the universal flood that is recorded in Genesis.[6] Therefore, a major flaw exists in the worldview based in the scientific rationalism of the Enlightenment. Presuppositions that have been falsely declared as fact have no doubt contributed to the distrust of many scientific claims that continue to be presently made. The scientist always forms his or her hypothesis with the belief that it might be the correct one, even though experimentation often proves it to have been a false one. As an experimental scientist, I never formed a hypothesis that I did not think might prove true. In the course of my professional scientific work, I once formed a hypothesis—regarding the nature of rubber friction—based on previously published scientific work. But after extensive experimentation, I had to change my hypothesis because the previously published scientific "facts" were faulty, even though they had

---

5. Hume, *Enquiry*, 458.

6. Since the biblical account of the universal flood of Noah is an accurate account of reality, any scientific worldview that does not account for that fact will be in error because it will assume a uniformity to nature that does not in fact exist. The earth's climatic conditions before that cataclysmic event were different from what they are today. The fact that crude oil, which is essentially decayed vegetation, is drilled from locations where that growth is not now supported testifies to the fact that significant changes in the earth's climate have occurred. Furthermore, the fact that atmospheric conditions before the flood were not capable of producing the rainbow is strong evidence to support this fact. A rainbow can only form when there is a unique interaction of light refraction and reflection with water in the atmosphere. Other evidence, apart from the appearance of the rainbow, is found in the shortening of life expectancy. UV rays are known to contribute greatly to the aging effect. Scripture teaches that after the flood, human life expectancy began a definite decline. Furthermore, the geological record all over the world points to a catastrophic event that brought many forms of life suddenly to an end, which strongly concurs with a universal flood event.

been represented as fact in a major scientific journal.[7] Experimentation, observation, and subsequent reason will prove a scientific hypothesis—or presupposition—to be either valid or faulty. A faulty hypothesis, should give rise to a better hypothesis, and this cycle, of course, is repeated until a given hypothesis has been confirmed, and thus scientific knowledge is advanced.

But the crucial point that I am making in this discussion of the scientific method is for the reader to realize that observation of natural phenomena, be it with the naked senses or one aided by the awe-inducing instruments now so prevalent in science, and subsequent theoretical speculation to conclusion, is simply not the scientific method. That may be the basis of legitimate hypotheses, but unless proper experimentation, complete with experimental controls, can be put into place, conclusions based on mere observation and subsequent speculation can be faulty and misleading. For example, distant starlight does not actually prove the age of the universe, because there cannot exist any controlled experiments that will ensure certainty about the conditions under which that starlight was initially generated and the conditions which may have ensued after that mysterious event which brought that star into existence. It is the simple mind that thinks that distant starlight absolutely proves the age of the universe. The whole concept of time is, as Einstein proved with his laws of relativity, a quantity which is relative to space and gravity, and both entities were far from anything near uniformity at the beginning of the universe.[8]

It is interesting to note some of the error filled reasoning which atheistic humanists, both Modern and Postmodern, often resort to in their attempt to justify their atheistic beliefs. While atheism in Western culture has failed to capture dominance in the general populace, it is interesting to consider why it yet dominates in academia. The academic community prides itself with a total reliance upon logic to form the foundation for all argument. They try to frame all their arguments in a light which appeals to reason. Both the academic atheist and the Postmodern existentialist will often put forth the argument that because religion is a primary source of world conflict and violence, the rational person would best hold to either an atheistic viewpoint or one which is indifferent to whether or not God

7. Carter, "Re-evaluation," 1283–86.

8. It is for this same reason that creation scientists can error when they attempt to quantify the age of the universe. At the creation event, the beginning of both time and space were an effect of that event. Einstein's theory of relativity must be taken into consideration when considering that event, with the knowledge that time loses all linearity under the conditions that must have then prevailed.

exists. A. C. Grayling hints at this argument in the opening lines of his *The God Argument* where he writes with amazing hyperbole:

> History attests to the weight of suffering that religious tyranny and conflict have together generated, from individuals struggling with feelings of sinfulness because of perfectly natural desires, to nations and civilizations engulfed in war and atrocity by inter-religious hatred. Religions have often been cruel in their effects, and remain so today; homosexuals are hanged in Iran, adulterous women are beheaded in Afghanistan and stoned to death in Saudi Arabia, 'witches' are murdered in Africa, women and children are subordinated in fundamentalist households in the Bible Belt of the United States and in many parts of the Islamic world. Throughout history the religion-inspired suppression of woman has robbed humanity of at least half its potential creativity and genius.[9]

Likewise, throughout his career Dawkins has appealed to this same argument. Dawkins has posited that the existence of God is less likely because of the violent conflict that religious belief has often fostered throughout history. But instead of this argument being a fresh and original one—i.e., as a valid impetus for believing that God does not exist because of the strife that belief in God generates—it is an argument that has been around for over 100 years. Flint tells us that it was in France where the idea became popular that religion was the primary cause of war, and hence, it was believed by many in France that the universal rise of atheism, or at least an indifference to any type allegiance to a personal God, would allow for world-wide peace. In response to this argument, Flint, showing his particularly keen mind, wrote in response to this faulty reasoning:

> Well, of course, if there were no religion people could not fight about it. But, obviously, they might still fight about other things, and even fight about them more frequently and ignobly than they do at present, just because of the absence of religion. Dogs have no religion, but they quarrel over a bone. Take away from man all interests and motives higher than those of a beast, and you do not thereby secure that he will be peaceable; on the contrary you ensure that he will quarrel as a beast and not as a man.[10]

---

9. Grayling, *The God Argument*, 1. This excerpt from Grayling also shows his biased hatred and ignorance for what he refers to as "fundamentalist," and particularly well demonstrates how the term has been twisted by humanists into something that it does not mean.

10. Flint, *Anti-Theistic*, 85.

A good example that demonstrates the validity of Flint's argument in current Postmodern American society can be seen in the loss of life and violent confrontation that occurred in May of 2015. In Waco, Texas a conflict between two rival motorcycle gangs claimed the lives of nine people and injured many others. Certainly, there was no place for religious faith in either party. To say that the primary cause of violent conflict in human relations is due to religious belief is, simply to have a very ignorant view of human nature. It should be apparent to the rational mind that conflict is the result of any human agency that wishes to impose its will over a co-existing entity that does not wish to have another's will imposed upon it. The concern of whether or not that imposition of will is justified, or not, does not need to be considered to see the presence of violent conflict. To claim as fact that wars fought because of differing religious beliefs yields evidence that there is no God, is simply ludicrous. Thus, atheistic humanistic reasoning results in illogical argument because it denies what is real.

While the Modern humanist likes to base his argument on the foundation of human reason, the Postmodern humanist is not so concerned about the strict rules of logic. The Secular existentialist will not resist the preceding argument for questioning the existence of God. However, his motivation for any belief lies in simply the will to believe based upon what he wishes for what he perceives as his own good. In summing up this section, I must stress that while there is, without doubt, genuine epistemological authority in the function of science, that authority is only valid where reproducible experiment can prove its contentions. When all is said and done, the philosophy of naturalism lies outside of rigorous scientific proof because it is full of hypotheses which cannot be proven by the scientific method. Scientific authority cannot be used to prove the philosophy of naturalism, although philosophers such as Richard Dawkins are diligently trying to put their atheistic beliefs into that authority.

Notwithstanding the superficial reason of the argument regarding violent conflict and religious belief, and those like it, the ultimate reason that atheism often prevails in academia is due to the pride of self-determination that is generated in the hearts of those who wish to throw off the authority of any entity that would interfere with that self-determination. In Isaiah 53, we read that all humanity has "gone astray" and every person "has turned to his own way." Furthermore, the well-known verses from the Psalms where it states that "the fool has said in his heart, there is no God" is actually better rendered "the fool has said in his heart, no God." In other words, "the fool" is proclaiming that there will be no God for him, instead of proclaiming that God does not exist.[11] It is this interpretation that better describes the unbelief of the Postmodern era. Therefore, the humanistic mind wills to discard the authority of Scripture in favor of an authority of science in support of evolutionary theories of the origin of man, which purposefully denies the existence of God. Note the emphasis here is on human volition. The will, as Nietzsche proclaimed, should reign over reason and this is the primary driving force in the epistemological shift to Postmodern thought.

To further show that the philosophy of naturalism is giving way to one of Existentialism, particularly within the general populace, I will mention another observation that I found to be exceedingly interesting. After watching a debate between an anti-evolutionist Christian and a popular scientist who was representing his case for atheistic naturalism with much hyperbole, I went online to see how the audience would respond to the arguments presented. I was surprised to see many Postmodern existentialistic responses that illustrated to me just how Postmodern Existentialism is slowly whittling away at the Enlightenment philosophy of naturalism. One reader on a journalistic website voicing his opinion regarding the debate responded as follows: "Any person that claims to know anything that happened before (ca.) 2,000 BC is a liar. Let's be honest with ourselves about what we don't know. Yes, there is evidence for evolution – but most of the details are as made up as the 7-day creation myth and the Bible's 4,000 BC chronology where people lived for 900 years. Yes, things evolve and early human skeletons are very different than those of today. But that's about it. Any scientist claiming to have a fully detailed evolutionary chain that stretches back to single cell organisms is a liar."

Whenever I read this response it always provokes in me a smile. While the responder was serious, the posting is nonetheless somewhat comical. It is thoroughly representative of an existentialistic worldview where the writer shows little concern for basing his thinking on a firm epistemological foundation. It is apparent that this poster could really care less about understanding how physical reality came into existence. While his response shows a particular ignorance of history—for there is much certainty of innumerable historical facts before 2000 BC—he nonetheless is perceptive enough to realize that much of what is claimed today in the name of science is simply rubbish.

11. Ps 14:1, Ps 53:1.

Scriptural Authority

Because of the historic clash between science and the church, science has sometimes been *wrongly* questioned by some Christians as a legitimate means to the formation of a valid epistemology. This is particularly true of those Christians who are suspect of higher education in general, primarily because of the methods of "higher criticism" which originated in the Protestant seminaries of Germany during the late period of the Enlightenment. The resulting "modernistic" theologies, which have traditionally denied the supernatural aspects of Scripture, eventually found their way into nearly all of the Protestant seminaries of Western culture. Of course, that faulty scholarship is still being produced and filtered down into the mainline Protestant seminaries, and this has resulted in many unbiblical teachings which has enabled humanistic philosophies to prevail within the mainline Christian churches of Western culture. Because of that so-called scholarship stemming from Enlightenment ideology many of these mainline churches now deny the supernatural inspiration of Scripture, and that denial, of course, is an attempt to strip Scripture of its supernatural authority. Because of the Apostle Paul's letter to the Colossians (2:3) where Christ is rightfully declared the final authority for all knowledge, many conservative theologians unfortunately have a dim view of science for serving as a legitimate role in the formation of a worldview which is epistemologically sound.

But while science nonetheless should be part of a sound philosophy and epistemology, it is limited in its stand-alone ability to give a correct worldview because of the transcendent nature of God. Because of the necessity for understanding his transcendent nature, God commanded His chosen people, the descendants of Abraham, Isaac, and Jacob to refrain from any type of idol worship. The stone and wood god-images of the surrounding pagan nations had nothing to do with the actual God of creation. Therefore, the ancient nation of Israel was commanded by their God not to worship any "graven image" because those images were false gods that were physically integral with the creation, i.e., the material cosmos. The fact that the punishment for violating this commandment was so severe, reflects the importance of understanding the transcendent nature of the creator. For example, the account of the Israelites worshiping the golden calf as recorded by Moses in Exodus shows this very well. Thus, the understanding of the transcendent nature of God is still an important prerequisite for gaining a genuine knowledge of ultimate reality, and thus, for forming a worldview that is real and true.

The fact of God's transcendence, however, does not mean that the knowledge of God's existence lies outside of a view of reality that is epistemologically sound or one that is within the realm of reason. It is important to note that Greek philosophy did not look to divorce rational thought from a reality separate from the phenomenology arising from the physical reality of the universe. Plato's philosophy left the door open for the wisdom of a transcendent God, and thus, Greek philosophy certainly played a role in preparing the Western gentile mind for the rational acceptance of the transcendent God of Hebrew and Greek Scripture. Therefore, metaphysical knowledge is a legitimate subject of epistemology. But because of God's transcendence, questions about both his existence and his nature lie outside the realm of scientific discovery. The scientific method, through reproducible experimentation, can only probe existing conditions of *physical* reality. Because of this fact science will never uncover a complete understanding of the mechanisms that brought about the beginning of matter, time, and space, that which we commonly refer to as the universe or the cosmos. The God of Hebrew Scripture is not a pantheistic God, and thus, God is not physically integral to phenomenological reality.[12] Therefore, a worldview based only in the authority of science, with no regard for the authority of Scripture, is one that can only give a faulty view of that which is real. Scripture tells us that the universe had a beginning, and science is confirming that truth, but science stops there because that beginning had a transcendent cause which is not subject to scientific examination. But before we deal with the validity of supernatural revelation, i.e., the validity of the revelation of Scripture, we must first deal with the natural revelation of God's existence, the revelation which will give all who have ever lived no excuse for their denial of God when they leave this life and pass into the reality of the transcendent.

How can we say with certainty that this transcendent God of which we speak lives? The simple answer to that question, primarily, is because the natural evidence of God's existence is so strong that it cannot be refuted. God has never asked anyone to disregard the gift of reason. A major error of Kierkegaard's Existentialism was his insistence that Christian faith is a great "leap," which in my mind implies a leap in the dark. But nothing could be further from the truth. William James, the noted American psychologist/

---

12. This argument is somewhat mitigated when considering any genuine miracle, especially the miracle of the Incarnation or even the miracle of the "new birth" spoken of by Jesus in John 3.

philosopher who wrote in the Modern era commented wisely about that which we are here discussing. He wrote, "What, in short, has authority to debar us from trusting . . . [in the existence of God] . . . ? Science as such assuredly has no authority, for she can only say what is [i.e., attest to the phenomenological reality of the cosmos], not what is not [i.e., cannot attest to anything outside of phenomenological reality]: and the agnostic 'thou shalt not believe without coercive sensible evidence' is simply an expression (free to anyone to make) of private personal appetite for evidence of a certain peculiar kind."[13] Because we are told in Scripture that all who have ever lived will be held without excuse before God, it must be that God has provided enough *natural* evidence of himself to make reasonable that accountability. The apostle Paul in his letter to the Romans wrote: "For since the creation of the world His invisible attributes, that is, His eternal power and divine nature, have been clearly perceived, being understood by what has been made, so that they are without excuse."[14]

The acquisition of all knowledge begins with presupposition, and this applies to the metaphysical knowledge of God's existence. All of us know that scientists begin their inquiry into physical truth with a presupposition known as the hypothesis. However, no matter the field of knowledge, a seeker of truth always begins with presupposition. Even a young child begins his learning experience with presupposition. Let a two-year-old toddler practice sitting in a toy plastic chair that is designed to hold his weight and he will most probably form the belief, through subconscious presupposition, that any chair-like structure of similar appearance will support him. If an identical chair constructed of cheap cardboard is put in front of him, he will no-doubt act (experiment) on that presupposition and will park his little body in that flimsy structure only to experience total collapse. Through a process of presupposition (or hypothesis), experiment, results, and then rational conclusion, he will learn that not all structures which are shaped like a chair, share the same function even though they might *appear* to be identical. And of course, his education on the mechanics of chair structure is only just beginning. He might someday learn that a cardboard chair could indeed be engineered that would be capable of holding his weight.[15]

13. James, *Essays*, 25, (parenthesis and interior quotation marks are James's, brackets are mine).

14. Rom 1:20.

15. See Appendix for further discussion of this example.

I have seen first-hand a similar scenario. My son and his family were visiting my home when my toddler grandson spotted a big beautiful red "apple" on a living-room desktop. No sooner than his eyes had latched onto the "apple," he was making a "bee-line" to the object to get a taste of the red ripe "fruit." He had formed in his little mind the presupposition that he was about to enjoy the taste of a delicious red apple. What he did not know, however, was that what he thought was an "apple" was a beautiful red designer candle which only had the appearance of an apple. He carried out his experiment when he took his first bite, and readily observed, i.e., discovered or learned, that not all objects that look like apples are apples. It was amusing to watch the learning experience take place. From the look on his little face after that first bite, the wax of which the apple was fashioned obviously had an unpleasant taste. He carried out an experiment when he took that first bite, and the result of that experiment is what gave him added knowledge of physical reality.

The acknowledgment of all truth, including that truth which lies outside the realm of the cosmos, involves an algorithm like the process just described, with the example of how even a child attains knowledge of the natural world. That algorithm is the same process which is involved in the scientific process, but, of course, that knowledge must by necessity exclude the knowledge which is derived from physical experimentation. Knowledge of the metaphysical yet involves presupposition, evidence, and conclusion. As in the case of the scientific hypothesis, the presupposition regarding God's existence comes from a rational process, no matter what Richard Dawkins wants his hearers to believe. The observed complexity of the universe, especially the complexity of the human body which every human mind possesses, should prompt—in a reasonable mind—the presupposition of an intelligent creator.

Anyone with a basic knowledge of the biochemistry involved in the existence and functioning of the human body must marvel at the profound details of the chemistry of life. However, even those who have earned the PhD in biochemistry have only rudimentary knowledge of the entirety of the biochemical mechanisms that necessitate life. But consider a complex entity which does not even *slightly* approach in magnitude the complexity of the human body. When one sees the complexity of the ordinary home computer one must suppose that a designer or a group of designers created it. The computer obviously did not just evolve into being, but it, of necessity, had to have been brought into existence by an intelligent entity. The presupposition that the universe had a beginning, and therefore has an intelligent cause behind its appearance is not an irrational hypothesis but a perfectly rational one. And it is at this point where the element of faith comes to bear on the realization of a worldview which is in fact based upon truth.

Because the presupposition of God's existence cannot be verified through the methods of science, the fact of his existence must first be accepted based on faith. In the supernaturally inspired letter written to the Hebrews the writer states: "And without faith it is impossible to please Him, for the one who comes to God must believe that He exists, and that He proves to be One who rewards those who seek Him."[16] It is obvious that before one can acknowledge the authority of Scripture one must believe that God exists. That is always the first step in coming to a worldview based in truth, and the point that I am trying to get across is the fact that this first step is not a leap in the dark but it is completely within the realm of reason. In fact, when considering the awe-inspiring complexity of nature, it is irrational to refuse to believe in a transcendent creator. Thus, the materialistic atheist who tries to base his atheism in the authority of science, plays the part of the hypocrite because he has formed his denial of God's existence without the coercive scientific evidence to which he appeals to as the basis for the source of all his knowledge. The "coercive sensible evidence" that the atheist appeals to is, in reality, actually less authoritative than is the "coercive sensible evidence" to which the one who holds to the belief in the transcendent creator. The ultimate questions of existence are outside the realm of scientific experimentation, and hence these questions must rely on evidence that cannot be used as proof based in the scientific method. But the "coercive sensible evidence" for the existence of the God of Hebrew and Greek Scripture abounds throughout the phenomenological world through the witness of nature, archeology, and personal testimony, and far outweighs the evidence that exists based on Darwin's theories for a universe that evolved from nothing or even the theories that guess that the universe has always existed. And this brings us to the goal of this discourse, which is to show the rational basis for the absolute authority of Scripture, and the fact that if one is to hold to a worldview based in truth, the absolute authority of Scripture must be acknowledged. But before we go there, let us return to the example from the first chapter where we left the question open of whether or not God will hold the one who has never heard the name of Jesus responsible for his or her rejection of God.

16. Heb 11:6.

Many will claim—perhaps even some Christians with an existentialis-tic bent who have a faulty understanding of the natural human heart—that a just God could never condemn one who has never heard the gospel of Jesus Christ, despite the fact that the evidence of creation itself is such that no rational person can deny the existence of a creator. But this natural evidence will be sufficient to render all who deny the existence of God without excuse when they come face to face with him when they leave this life. Even in the Hebrew Scripture we find a subtle address of this difficult dilemma. In Deuteronomy we read of a principle that, while addressed specifically to the Israelites at the time it was written, can be taken as a principle that applies to all people today. It reads: "But from there you will seek the Lord your God, and you will find Him if you search for Him with all your heart and all your soul."[17] In other words, Scripture is here saying that the one who comes to the point of genuinely desiring in his heart (or his very-most true inner-being) to come to a knowledge of the God of creation, that one will indeed find that God will be faithful in somehow revealing himself, and thereby the Christ, to that one. (After all it is the sovereign God who has put that desire in the non-believer's heart in the first place.)

Therefore, most all people acknowledge that some type of "ulti-mate mover," or supreme being must exist based solely on the profound complexity of nature. Plato and Aristotle both held to the existence of a transcendent supreme being, due to the premise that the existence of God is self-evident through the obvious, but certainly profound, complexity of nature. King David described it particularly well when he stated that "The heavens declare the glory of God and the firmament showeth forth his handiwork."[18] However, it is safe to say that while the atheism based in the rationalism of Enlightenment Humanism is in decline, the atheism based in Existentialism is on the rise in Western culture. I recently read in Wikipedia—not always the best source for reliable information—that the population of Germany is approaching the 50 percent mark where there are as many atheists as there are theists.

But clearly a vast majority of those people who submit to the fact of God's existence stop short of acknowledging the fact that God has made himself known through the pages of the Hebrew and Greek Scripture. These spend their lives searching in vain, through man-made systems of re-ligion, for evidence that will give credence to their belief in God's existence.

17. Deut 4:29.
18. Ps 119:1 (KJV).

That quest for truth often ends in disappointment because these have often failed to realize the necessity of an authoritative source for metaphysical truth. A genuine knowledge of the God of creation simply cannot be arrived at outside of the supernatural revelation of both the Hebrew and Greek Scripture. The fact that Hebrew Scripture accurately foretold of the long-awaited Jewish Messiah should convince anyone of Scripture's truth. But the recognition of that knowledge is contingent upon the perceiver truly wishing deep within his or her being to know the truth about the God of creation. Hebrew Scripture foretold of Jesus's virgin birth, the very town in which he would be born, and foretold of even his death and resurrection.

However, despite these facts, unfortunately, both Modern and Postmodern humanists often insist that the biblical record of history either be accepted as a mythological source or as a source of information which has little bearing on the existential reality of everyday life. But it is only an epistemology which can acknowledge Scripture as the authoritative source of all metaphysical truth, which will give the knowledge that leads to a worldview based in truth. As we previously discussed regarding the Holocaust of WWII, the contention that millions of Jews were murdered by the Nazi Third Reich is either true or false, and the truth of that matter does not depend upon what anyone might or might not believe about it. Even if most people in existence believed that the Holocaust never happened, that belief would have no outcome on the fact that it indeed did happen as history records it. Likewise, the God of the Hebrew and Greek Scriptures either speaks with authority through that Scripture or he does not. The fact that most people might not believe that Jesus is the Christ does not change the fact that he is the Christ. How can anyone know the truth regarding either matter?

The most convincing evidence that the Scriptures speak authoritatively to metaphysical reality is in the fact of Jesus's resurrection from the dead. As the apostle wrote to the Greek Christians at Corinth in the first century "and if Christ has not been raised, then our preaching is in vain, your faith also is in vain."[19] If the claim that Jesus is a myth were to be true then this book too is in vain and so are the lives of every Christian who has ever lived. In fact, if Jesus is a myth then all lives are in vain, and all of us should claim the Existentialism of Sartre as our philosophy. Our knowledge of Jesus, who he was, from where he came, and the purpose for his coming, is rooted in the authority of Scripture. *Why should it be difficult to recognize that the God who brought everything that exists into being could not,*

19. 1 Cor 15:14.

or would not, convey the nature of his being to his creation? The Scripture gives us eyewitness accounts as to what he taught, how he lived, how he died, and the assurance that he arose the third day after his crucifixion. There are many eyewitness accounts, from reputable and credible sources, to the many things that Jesus said and did during his short life near and in Jerusalem about 2000 years ago. The Scriptures are replete with the reports of both his many activities and his many spoken words. But despite the inspired words of Scripture, it is not uncommon today to find authors who question whether or not Jesus was even a historical person! The question of Jesus's actual existence is also either true or false. Jesus, who was crucified by the Roman government, either existed or He did not exist. It cannot go both ways. The Postmodern, so-called scholars, who suggest that Jesus is a mythical figure, do so because they simply will to believe that falsehood, and not because there is a genuine preponderance of the evidence in support of their belief.[20] These so-called scholars simply will not accept the authority of Scripture. It is indeed amazing how anyone could refuse to acknowledge the truth of Jesus's existence, when after he was crucified by Roman authorities, he rose from the tomb and appeared to all his close associates and even appeared to as many as 500 others who bore testimony to the truth of that resurrection.[21] How much more evidence should one require to accept the fact that Jesus was the Christ?

In the following chapter I will show how faulty interpretations of nature can easily prevail when Scripture is not acknowledged as a true accounting of reality. For forming the presupposition that the uniformity of nature was changed in a major way by the universal flood of Noah described in Genesis, the authority of Scripture must come into play. If one cannot believe that the rainbow first appeared after that event, as Scripture very plainly states, or if one cannot trust the accuracy of the lengthy life-spans that Scripture claims to have existed before that great universal flood, then the presupposition that the flood event brought about a major change in the earth's atmosphere where UV radiation became more intense, becomes less likely. In fact, that presupposition becomes nearly impossible if one refuses to acknowledge that the flood was universal in scope as the

---

20. The effect of this Postmodern trend is even witnessed in our Western systems of criminal justice. Many people have been convicted of serious crimes, and even sentenced to death with essentially no convincing evidence because of a prosecutor's (and jury's) will to do so. Likewise, many people who are genuinely guilty have been exonerated based solely on the jury's will to set them free.

21. 1 Cor 15:6.

Scripture declares it to have been. Of course, the refusal to believe that the uniformity of nature was interrupted by the great flood is the position that materialistic atheists must hold to. The current theories of human evolution require the assumption of a uniformity of nature that is presumed to have existed for multiple billions of years. There is no scientific proof for this assumption. Wherever the archaeological record of a massive flood is irrefutable, the Modern humanistic scientists simply claim that the evidence merely points to a local catastrophe and not the universal flood that was supernaturally revealed to Moses.[22] In the next chapter I will offer irrefutable evidence, which Postmodern science is suppressing, that there was a substantial change in the uniformity of nature which occurred during the time of that great flood.

22. Keller, *Bible as History*, 43–49.

7

The Deceit of Postmodern Science

THE PRIMARY DEVELOPMENT WHICH gave rise to the false optimism of the Modern era was the countless number of successful applications resulting from scientific discovery. Those innumerable discoveries, and their application in every discipline of scientific knowledge imaginable, drastically changed the entire character of Western culture by enabling the belief that scientific discovery could, and most likely would, provide the means for mankind to independently control both his environment and his destiny. However, the realization that science had opened the door to the total extermination of all humankind was, most probably, a contributing factor in the advent of the Postmodern Existentialism that we are here considering. And while technological advancements are yet continuing at an unprecedented pace, those advancements are serving to reinforce the Postmodern conviction that science will never bring to the human condition the peace, contentment, meaning, and purpose of which all human beings are seeking. Postmodern Western culture is now well characterized, and understandably so, by mistrust in many of the claims that have been—and are now being made—in the name of science. All of this is not to say that the false optimism in science that once was once highly prevalent in the Western Modern mindset has entirely faded from the reality of contemporary thinking. That false optimism still exists, although it has been corralled and limited to the Modern derived Humanism that now has less influence in the educated populace of Western culture than it once did.

My early primary, and secondary education was in the setting of a high-quality public educational system where that Modern humanistic mindset was well entrenched. I vividly remember a classroom setting in 1961, where, as a class, we watched Alan Shepherd being blasted into outer space. We were told by our teacher that the goal of humans landing on the moon was within the reach of the then-current technology. I was in awe of that statement, and there was no doubt in my mind that the teacher was proclaiming truth. This was a time in history when technology was exploding at breakneck speed. If that same teacher had then told the class that science would someday supply the knowledge to allow for indefinite lengths of human life, I at that young impressionable age, would have accepted that hypothesis as a practical one. There is no doubt that that humanistic educational system was instilling in me the Modern humanistic mindset which viewed science as the ultimate determiner of reality. I remember going home and mentioning at the dinner table that it was very probable that humans would soon walk on the moon. My father made the comment, in his usual dogmatic manner, that that would never happen, and when that event did in fact occur a mere eight years later, this episode was influential in causing me to reject the Christianity of my childhood, and put me on a path which would take me away from the Christian commitment that I had made early in life. The false optimism of Modern Humanism was certainly influencing my young developing mind. While my dear father was wrong in this instance, he certainly had the wisdom to understand that human knowledge would never even closely approach the infinite knowledge of the creator who set the entire universe in motion through the power of his Word.

As I have pointed out repeatedly in my writing, while Postmodern Existentialism has certainly blunted the power of this false optimism, it is nonetheless still working in Western culture. As the reader has by now no doubt surmised, I am fond of giving specific examples to show first-hand the truth claims that I bring to bear in this discussion of Postmodern Existentialism. As unbelievable as it may seem, there are scientists today who are making the claim that within the timespan of only a few more years, science will supply the knowledge which will enable humans to live indefinitely. The British tabloid *The Sun*, in early 2020, published an article featuring the claims of Dr. Ian Pearson, where he purported that by the year of 2050 science will be within the reach of achieving human immortality. The article began with the words:

"If you're under 40 reading this article, you're probably not going to die unless you get a nasty disease." Those are the words of esteemed futurologist Dr. Ian Pearson, who told The Sun he believes humans are very close to achieving "immortality" – the ability to never die.[1]

When I first read the article, my immediate impression was that this had to be an example of the typical irresponsible reporting that is often observed in Postmodern journalism, where the importance of rational reporting is commonly overlooked for the sake of commercial gain. At first, I even questioned the legitimacy of Dr. Ian Pearson, but upon further investigation, much to my surprise, I found him to be a legitimate scientifically trained individual, who holds a scientific doctorate from the University of Westminster in London. Although his doctorate is not the PhD, his specialty appears to be as an advisor and lecturer to any organization that looks to gain firsthand knowledge as to the accomplishments that science will give in both the near and distant future. A listing of his current and former clients includes some of the most powerful and successful organizations in the corporate world.

Unfortunately, however, I have unwelcome news for Dr. Pearson and all his important clients, corporate and otherwise, who will hear me. I will even take on the same dogmatism that my father incorrectly assumed when he denied that man would walk on the moon, without any fear whatsoever that I might be wrong as was he 60 years ago. I do not give this proclamation in the authority of my own scientific education, but I give it on the authority of Scripture. That proclamation is this: "There will never be a scientific achievement or discovery that will prevent human death." Scripture states with absolute authority: "And just as it is destined for people to die once, and after this comes judgment, . . ."[2] and "the Scripture cannot be broken."[3] Dr. Pearson's projections have provided evidence that the optimism of the Secular Humanism that proceeded from Enlightenment reasoning is still operational, and furthermore, proves why the Enlightenment worldview is losing ground to the Postmodern worldview, a worldview which understands that science can often no longer be trusted because of its claims which are sometimes not in the realm of reality.

Therefore, I can say with certainty that much of what today is being passed off as science is nothing more than untested, or more commonly,

1. Keach, "Live Forever," paras. 1–2.
2. Heb 9:27.
3. John 10:35.

poorly tested hypotheses. Moreover, often legitimate scientific hypotheses are simply refused to be entertained by Postmodern scientists because of the possibility of an experimental outcome that might prove the existence of preconceived biases on viewpoints having a philosophical bent which prevail within the academic community. Any subject which might shine light on the truth of Scripture, particularly in the disciplines of archeology, geology, and history, will not get the support of unbiased scientific inquiry in today's Postmodern climate. If any aspect of Scripture can be proven true through archeology and/or scientific discovery, then the scriptural account of the creator cannot simply be continued to be regarded as myth, as many humanistic scientists regard Scripture. Additionally, in our Postmodern institutions, often mere hypotheses are pronounced as fact, based on the sheer will to do so, because of the inability to test them by experiment.

The Scientific Misrepresentations in the Medical and Social Sciences

An entire book could readily be written from examples that show the use of biased science to achieve philosophical purposes. For example, in 2013 there appeared in the *Journal of the American Medical Association (JAMA) Internal Medicine* an article reporting on a recent study that showed that states with the most gun control laws were the states that had the fewer gun deaths. This conclusion was reached by including statistics on death by gun suicide, a fact which in essence destroys the credibility of the entire article, since the argument for increased gun legislation is to prevent violent crime, of which suicide statistics cannot be rationally included.[4] The study was obviously politically motivated in the aftermath of incidences of gun violence in the United States of America, which prompted liberal law makers to push for limiting public access to firearms, despite a constitutional guarantee that American citizens must have the right to bear arms. The study, which used data compiled by the liberal *Brady Center to Prevent Gun Violence*, was obviously seriously biased, and that study is a good example of using so-called scientific research to manipulate a view of reality that the researchers wished to purvey. Ironically, the study originated in Chicago, an amusing fact since Chicago has some of the strictest gun control laws in the country, yet has some of the nation's highest murder rates generated by gunfire. But to show how the masses have come to regard these

4. Fleegler, "Firearm Legislation," 732–40.

so-called scientific studies, one only needs to review the online comments contributed by the public when this story was reported via the on-line news media. One such response was "If you believe (these) studies, I've got some oceanfront property in Arizona I'd like to sell you." Another wrote, "Talk about cherry-picking your facts . . . This is absolutely . . . absurd." Numerous responses were in the vein of these two examples and they vastly outnumbered the responses that were favorable to the claims of the so-called scientific paper. This example is particularly keen for showing how the current Postmodern culture has exalted the importance of human volition over reason, and to think that it appeared in what is purported to be a leading Western scientific journal of internal medicine makes it a particularly good example to prove the point which I am making.

Moreover, perhaps an even more poignant example that demonstrates the negative effect that Postmodern Existentialism is having in the medical sciences is one that is in progress even as I write these words. I know of a person that was traveling in Buenos Aires in February of 2020 just before the Covid-19 pandemic became a world-wide issue. During that visit that person experienced a sickness, "like he had never before experienced," but because he was not aware of the soon to be viral pandemic, he had no way of associating his illness with the now well-known Covid-19 virus. He is convinced, based on his symptoms, that he had contracted the virus, but one that his immune system had successfully defended against. More than one year later, when the vaccine became available he asked his physician to test him for Covid-19 antibodies. Much to his surprise his physician stated that antibody testing was against the policy of the major medical corporation for which he worked. He then met with road blocks at every attempt to get meaningful antibody testing. He found a concerted effort within the American medical establishment to discourage meaningful antibody testing, presumably because of the government's desire to vaccinate all Americans. Gaining knowledge of natural antibody formation was evidently not deemed to be of sufficient importance to over-ride the government's vaccination program.

And examples which include no political motivation for obscuring facts, coming from so-called scientific studies in the health sciences, are likewise legion. For example, not too long ago, health scientists were telling us that if one desired good health, his or her breakfast should include neither butter or the yolk of the ubiquitous chicken egg, or for that matter, even coffee. This even though all these popular breakfast components have, since the history of American culture, been staples of the American breakfast. It turns out that these recommendations were based on hypotheses that had not been sufficiently tested to be labeled as fact, since later scientific reports have seen reversals of all these original health claims. Of course, if these were isolated examples, it would hardly be worthy of mention, but a complete volume could no doubt be written on similar scientific claims coming from the literature of the various heath-sciences.[5]

Nonetheless, the desire to shape perceptions of reality through manipulation of facts is even more pronounced in the social sciences. In my prior book I pointed out, in the introduction to the second chapter, that the social sciences offer a poor means to a true knowledge of human nature. The fact that human beings are created in the image of God puts human nature in a realm that is distinct from the purely physical nature of the universe. Since I made that proclamation, a study from the University of Virginia has given credence to my claim. From *Newsweek* in August, 2015, came the report that out of 100 published studies in the social sciences, not even half could be reproduced. Quoting *Newsweek*:

> For the project, researchers who had not worked on the original studies selected papers to test out that were published in three prominent journals: *Psychological Science*, the *Journal of Personality and Social Psychology* and the *Journal of Experimental Psychology: Learning, Memory, and Cognition*. The first is a premier outlet for all psychological research; the others are leading journals for social psychology and cognitive psychology.
> The researchers discovered they could replicate less than half of the original findings, which raises the question of how the original researchers arrived at their conclusions (and formed their hypotheses) in the first place.[6]

Even the subject of history is now susceptible to the manipulation of facts in the interest of those who are simply willing to perpetuate a desired perception, even if that perception is based in falsehood. Again, I will use the example of the Jewish Holocaust to point out this Postmodern trend. The hate for the Jewish people in some cultures is so intense that some educators are now trying to change the perception of truth, regarding the tragedy of Holocaust of World War II, simply through sheer willpower. There are those

5. Interestingly, I read of a scientific research program currently in progress where the researchers are claiming that Facebook profiles can be used to diagnose mental illnesses.

6. Firger, "Reproducibility Problem," paras. 4–5.

who claim that the Holocaust is mostly myth, insisting that it did not happen as most textbooks of Western history have correctly portrayed it.

But it is in the study of the origin of the universe, and the life therein, where some of the most blatant abuses of science are occurring. There is a growing tendency in the study of the origins of the universe to simply disregard any evidence which might cast any doubt whatsoever on current evolutionary teachings which most secular humanistic scientists dogmatically insist accurately accounts for the origin of man. With increasing instances of misleading claims in the name of science, a de-emphasis in the historical scientific method—in favor of the sheer "will-to-power" that is exhalated in the work of Nietzsche—has become dominant in Postmodern Western culture. Evidence which points to the truth of Scripture and to the discredit of current-day teachings of the origins of human life is often simply willed to be non-existent by materialistic atheistic scientists. But before going forward to consider an example that particularly gives evidence to this bold claim, we will first consider evidence that some contemporary medical doctors have recently brought to light in metaphysics.

The medical sciences are unique, in that within this discipline of science there is a unique meeting of the physical with the metaphysical. Soul and body are connected in a mysterious union to which only the revelation of Scripture can effectively lend understanding. Unfortunately, the training that most physicians have received during their medical education, has consisted of pre-med programs which mandate courses in human evolution. It would be difficult to obtain an undergraduate degree in biology, in most universities, without significant exposure to biological evolution. Thus, most contemporary practicing physicians in the Western world, have been taught to believe that humans evolved from a single cell, a cell that came into existence billions of years ago through the random combination of carbon dioxide, methane, oxygen, and nitrogen gases to, eventually, yield the basic chemical building blocks of life. As such, a majority of practicing physicians in Western culture are of an atheistic persuasion. However, despite these disturbing facts, some practicing physicians currently active in the medical sciences have supplied compelling evidence that individual consciousness survives the death of the body, which of course, again lends itself to the metaphysical conclusion, derived from Scripture, that human death does not end existence as materialistic atheists and atheistic existentialists suppose.[7]

---

7. The reader is cautioned not to infer from near-death experiences any other knowledge than the fact that they give evidence that human consciousness survives the death

Dr. Melvin Morse (M.D.), a pediatric surgeon, authored a book where he documented the experiences of children who were clinically declared dead, but who, because of advanced resuscitation techniques, subsequently had breathing and circulation restored.[8] Despite Morse's desire to get the phenomenon of near-death experiences documented in the medical literature, he was thoroughly rebuffed by the medical journals for even trying to open his findings to scientific discussion. Even more recently, Dr. Mary Neal (M.D.) wrote of her near-death experience when she was trapped underwater in a kayaking accident for more than 30 minutes and had subsequently lost both respiration and circulation.[9] It is a fascinating read which again lends convincing evidence to the fact that every human being, as a creation in God's image, is in possession of a soul which will survive physical death. And finally, even more recently, Dr. Eben Alexander (M.D.), a practicing neurosurgeon, documented his near-death experience which he insisted was so real that it proved to him that human consciousness survives the death experience.[10]

The Mistreatment of Charles H. Hapgood

I present here two separate instances where the academic community has obscured the work of Charles H. Hapgood because, in both instances, his work opened the door for conclusions which have put current evolutionary based teachings of origins into disrepute. Hapgood was an obscure college professor, now deceased, who seemed to have been an independent thinker. He obtained both his undergraduate and graduate degrees from Harvard, and although he completed most of the requirements for the PhD, he did not complete his study possibly because of financial hardship brought on by the economic depression of 1929. It was perhaps the lack of that qualification, so crucial for proper recognition in all academic disciplines, which prompted his significant quest for contributing to the corpus of recognized knowledge.

Hapgood became intrigued by the fact that data being generated in the geological sciences was showing significant inconsistences in the understanding of the timelines concerning the ice formations of the ice age,

experience. About the only aspect of these near-death experiences that is consistently agreed upon is the fact that there is reality/consciousness beyond earthly or bodily existence.

8. Morse, *Closer to the Light*.

9. Neal, *Heaven and Back*.

10. Alexander, *Proof of Heaven*.

the study of which had become popular in academic geology in the postwar years. Hapgood, expressed reasonable concerns that geology was in a lost condition as far as dating the events of the ice age. Radiocarbon dating and other experimental results had begun to show dates that could not be reconciled with the time periods of the accepted storyline of academic geology. When Hapgood became aware that there was a strong possibility that the continent of Antarctica was, in very recent history, free of the icecap that now dominates the continent, he began to construct an "earth shifting crust" theory to account for the facts that were coming to light. He wrote:

> Some long cores . . . had been taken from the bottom of the Ross Sea in Antarctica by Dr. Jack Hough during the Byrd expedition of 1947–48. These cores showed alternations in types of sediment. There was coarse glacial sediment, as was expected, and finer sediment of semi glacial type, but there were also layers of fine sediment typical of temperate climates. It was the sort of sediment that is carried down by rivers from ice-free continents. Here was a first surprise, then. Temperate conditions had evidently prevailed in Antarctica in the not distant past.[11]

In 1958 Hapgood published *Earth's Shifting Crust: A Key to Some Basic Problems of Earth Science* to propose a theory of the earth's shifting crust which would account for the fact that at least parts of Antarctica had once, in the not-too-distant past, been ice free. Hapgood proposed that the continent of Antarctica had once been some 2000 miles (about the distance from Chicago to Los Angeles) north of its present location, which would have been a more temperate climate. The evidence was strong enough for Albert Einstein to endorse Hapgood's idea as a legitimate hypothesis. As stated by Einstein in his preface to Hapgood's book:

> I frequently receive communications from people who wish to consult me concerning their unpublished ideas. It goes without saying that these ideas are very seldom possessed of scientific validity. The very first communication, however, that I received from Mr. Hapgood electrified me. His idea is original, of great simplicity, and—if it continues to prove itself—of great importance to everything that is related to the history of the earth's surface. A great many empirical data indicate that at each point on the earth's surface that has been carefully studied, many climatic changes have taken place, apparently quite suddenly. This, according to Hapgood, is explicable if the virtually rigid outer crust of the earth undergoes, from time

11. Hapgood, *Crust*, 50.

to time, extensive displacement over the viscous, plastic, possibly fluid inner layers. Such displacements may take place as the consequence of comparatively slight forces exerted on the crust, derived from the earth's momentum of rotation, which in turn will tend to alter the axis of rotation of the earth's crust.[12]

It is important to note that Hapgood was proposing a theory which would have, in his estimation, supported the current understanding of Darwinian evolution. By suggesting that the earth's crust was shifting, he was trying to give credence to Darwin's theories which were then coming under attack, even in the scientific community. Hapgood delineated very carefully the scientific objections that were being raised regarding Darwin's theory of evolution. In closing the chapter where he discussed those issues raised against the Darwinian theory, he wrote:

> To sum up: it would seem that in crust displacements we have the missing factor that can bring all the other evolutionary factors into proper focus and correct perspective. By crust displacements we may accelerate the tempo of natural selection, provide the conditions of isolation and competition required for change in life forms, and account for periods of revolutionary change, for the distribution of species across oceans and climatic zones, and for the extinction of species. We may also account for the significant association of turning points in evolution with geological and climatic changes, presenting them as different results of the same cause. But for crust displacements to have had these effects, and if they are, indeed, to account for the evolution of species, they must have occurred very often throughout the history of the earth.[13]

But it was Hapgood's study of ancient maps which solidified his thinking that Antarctica in the not-too-distant past, i.e., sometime before 4000 BC, had been, at least partially, ice free. The study of the Piri Re'is map of 1513 further spurred his interest in proving that Antarctica had once been in a more temperate climate. Hapgood genuinely believed that finding would lend overwhelming credence to his theory that the earth's crust was shifting in significant magnitudes. What follows is a brief accounting of how this map came to the attention of Hapgood.

Piri Re'is was a Turkish admiral born at Gelibolu, a community on the Marmara Sea, sometime between the years of 1465 and 1470. At that time

12. Hapgood, *Crust*, 1.
13. Hapgood, *Crust*, 339.

Gelibolu (or Gallipoli) served as the naval base for the ships of the Ottoman empire.[14] Early in his life, Piri sailed extensively with his pirate uncle, Admiral Kemal Re'is. In his uncle's service he became skilled in navigation and cartography. It is reported that he came into possession of Christopher Columbus's map of America, sometime between the years 1493 and 1498.[15] Following his uncle's death, in battle, in 1511 on the open seas, Piri Re'is gave up sailing and began focusing his professional efforts on map-making.[16] In addition to creating a stand-alone map of the world, he authored a work known as *Kitab-i Bahriye*, (Book of the Sea). This work has been described as "a set of maps embedded in text that suggests travel guide, celebration of sovereignty, and work of art. Like other atlases of its time, it focuses on . . . fortresses, and physical features . . . ."[17]

Although the *Kitab-i Bahriye* is extant, Piri Re'is's primary notoriety now comes from the only extant portion of his world map dated 1513. That map depicts the coast lines of the Atlantic Ocean to include the Western coasts of Africa and Europe and the Eastern coasts of the Americas, primarily South America. The Piri Re'is map of 1513 was discovered during a re-ordering and inventory of the Imperial Palace of Constantinople in 1929. This discovery brought new excitement to the world of cartography mainly because the map was the earliest existing map of the Americas. But more importantly it was the first map to put the continent of Africa and South America into a proper longitudinal position. This is considered significant because in 1513 no technology to accomplish that endeavor was known to exist.[18]

Piri Re'is had included various legends on the map to supply information regarding the map's varied sources. In addition to his own cartography, the map was assembled from other sources that dated to very ancient times. One legend claims that the Western part of the map had its origins in the work of Columbus and another one showed that at least 20 source maps had been used, some of them dating to the time of Alexander the Great.[19]

In 1956 a copy of the map was given to the U.S. Navy Hydro-graphic Office as a gift from a Turkish naval officer, and the map eventually ended

14. Afetinan, *Life and Works*, 9.
15. Afetinan, *Life and Works*, 12.
16. Afetinan, *Life and Works*, 13.
17. Askan, *Ottomans*, 50.
18. Hapgood, *Sea Kings*, 1.
19. Hapgood, *Sea Kings*, 2.

up in the hands of retired U.S. Navy Captain Arlington H. Mallery. Mallery, a distinguished engineer, who was known for his interests in ancient maps, navigation, archeology, and his belief that Vikings had discovered the Americas long before did Columbus.[20] Captain Mallery was intrigued with the map's representations of the coastlines of the southern most regions of South America. Because the coastline trailed into eastern regions coinciding with the latitudes of Antarctica, it appeared that there was a possibility that the coastline of Antarctica had somehow been mapped. This suggestion by Mallery inspired Hapgood to take up an intensive study of the map. Hapgood was interested in knowing whether or not Mallery's hypothesis, regarding the mapping of the Antarctica coastline, had any possibility of being legitimate. During his investigation, he summoned the help of the U.S. Air Force. In the Air Force's response to Hapgood's inquiry, Lt. Colonel Ohlmeyer wrote the following in regards to the Piri Reis 1513 map:

> The claim that the lower part of the map portrays the Princess Martha Coast of Queen Maud Land Antarctica, and the Palmer Peninsula, is reasonable. We find this is the most logical and, in all probability, the correct interpretation of the map. The geographical detail shown in the lower part of the map agrees very remarkably with the results of the seismic profile made across the top of the ice-cap by the Swedish-British Antarctic Expedition of 1949. This indicates the coastline had been mapped before it was covered by the ice-cap. The ice-cap in this region is now about a mile thick. We have no idea how the data on this map can be reconciled with the supposed state of geographical knowledge in 1513.[21]

Hapgood, of course, was aware that if there was any possibility that the coastline of Antarctica had been mapped in ancient times, it would be contrary to the currently accepted understanding of geological history. He wrote:

> The importance of all this evidence is obvious when we realize that, as late as 1950, there appeared to be no question but that the icecap in Antarctica was millions of years old. According to Brooks, the geologists Wright and Priestly had presented conclusive evidence of the beginning of the present icecap as far back as the beginning of the Tertiary Period, some 60 or 80 million years ago. Now we have evidence of several periods of semi glacial or nonglacial

20. Hapgood, Sea Kings, 2, (Mallery may have formed that belief based upon the discovery of the Kensington Runestone, the authenticity of which is still being debated today).

21. Hapgood, Sea Kings, 243.

conditions in Antarctica in the Pleistocene Epoch alone. This is sufficient to show us how little reliance can be placed upon the estimated durations of hundreds of thousands or millions of years for the glacial periods of the remote past.[22]

Hapgood, however, was an objective researcher. His writing shows him to have been an intelligent and careful logician. Not resting on the success of the discovery of that one map, he searched for other ancient maps that might support the findings of the Piri Re'is map. In that search he found the Oronteus Fineaus map of 1531, and that map confirmed the findings of the Piri Re'is map. Hapgood documented those findings in his book, *Maps of the Ancient Sea Kings: Evidence of Advanced Civilization in the Ice Age.*[23]

While our purpose here is obviously not to present the details of Hapgood's study, our consideration here is to show the exceeding prejudices in the scientific community when any data is brought forth which refutes the so-called facts of the currently accepted evolutionary worldview. Hapgood's theory of the shifting earth's crust was rejected by the academic geological community, but in rejecting that theory it opened the door for lending significant credence to the universal worldwide flood which is recorded in Holy Scripture.

While Hapgood's theory of a shifting crust was rejected, Hapgood's findings nonetheless show there was a major worldwide climate change which coincided with the approximate time of the flood of Genesis, a fact that academic geology still refuses to acknowledge. Hapgood correctly realized that the data generated from modern dating methods proved that academic geology was wrong in most of the accepted understanding of the ice age. Hapgood so wisely wrote: [the data] "seems to challenge the principle laid down by the founder of modern geology, Sir Charles Lyell, over a century ago. Lyell's principle, called uniformitarianism, was that geological processes have always gone on about as they are going on now."[24] Science simply cannot ignore the cataclysmic event of the worldwide flood recorded in Scripture, of which there is much evidence, and conclude with a correct geological interpretation of the history of the earth. This is a fact that cannot be refuted.

22. Hapgood, *Crust*, 52.
23. Hapgood, *Sea Kings*, 243.
24. Hapgood, *Crust*, 48.

Apart from the afore-mentioned example, another interesting and significant example involves the same investigator, Charles H. Hapgood. Hapgood appears to be one who simply desired to pursue his discoveries wherever the evidence took him. And again, if one wants to see the desperate attempts displayed by those with a secular humanistic mind-set to destroy the credibility of any evidence that brings doubt to their worldview, one need only to peruse the Wiki encyclopedia article that deals with any subject where the so-called scientific subject of origins is challenged, to, of course, include this example.

The discovery of *Figurines of Acámbaro* revolve around an educated German hardware merchant named Waldemar Julsrud, who had made his home in Mexico many years earlier. This discovery was not simply a random and uninformed find. Julsrud was intimately familiar with the archaeological world and, no doubt, was primarily in Mexico because of his interest in early American history, particularly the history of American natives. Twenty years prior to the Acámbaro discovery, Julsrud and a local priest, in 1923, had discovered figurines and pottery fragments that became attributed to the Chupicaro culture. This culture was discovered from an archaeological site only a few miles from Acámbaro and has since been the subject of extensive excavating.[25]

But it was Julsrud's 1944 discovery of a vast collection of clay figurines that brings into question the credibility of scientific claims that the dinosaurs became extinct 65 million years ago. The clay figurines clearly depict the co-existence of dinosaurs and humans. And of course, because of these conclusions, the scientific world has simply claimed the findings to be a grand hoax engineered by either by Julsrud or his coworker who was responsible for the manual labor of retrieving the figurines from the earth. These charges came despite convincing evidence that points to the fact that Julsrud's discovery was a genuine archaeological find. There was simply zero evidence to lend credibility to the claims that the figurines, which give evidence to the fact that man and dinosaurs lived simultaneously, were manufactured, and planted in the ground to commit a hoax on the archaeological world. Anyone who honestly wants to probe the truth about this archaeological find will also come to this conclusion. Thus, Postmodern science and its archaeological sister have become impotent in maintaining objectivity for the purpose of shedding unbiased light on the truth of the history of the earth.

25. Hapgood, *Mystery*, 15,75.

Hapgood first visited Acámbaro in 1955, and along with Margaret Regler, confirmed that the findings were genuine representations of ancient Indian life.[26] In addition, Hapgood found actual animal teeth in the collection and wrote that he "later took these teeth to Dr. George Gaylord Simpson, America's leading paleontologist, at the Museum of Natural History. Dr. Simpson identified them as the teeth of *equus conversidans owen*, an extinct horse of the ice age."[27] Hapgood also had a working relationship with the well-known biologist Ivan T. Sanderson, and after Sanderson examined one of the figurines he wrote: "This figurine is in that very fine, jet-black, polished-looking ware. It is about a foot tall. The point is, it is an absolutely perfect representation of Brachiosaurus, known only from East Africa and *North America*. There are a number of outlines of the skeletons in the standard literature but only one fleshed-out reconstruction that I have ever seen. This statuette is exactly like it."[28]

In conclusion, a final word on the life and work of Mr. Charles Hapgood is in order. Hapgood is to be admired for courage in presenting his findings which went contrary to the yet prevailing storyline of geological and archeological history. Few, if any, contemporary graduate students, working for a graduate degree in the field of geology or archeology would have that courage which Hapgood displayed, because it would certainly mean that they would be expelled from their goal of obtaining an advanced degree. Certain aspects of both geology and archeology deal with the reconstruction of history, and these reconstructions can easily produce error-prone conclusions that the hard-physical sciences, such as pure chemistry and physics, are not subject to. I was fortunate to have chosen a scientific discipline that is grounded in objective truth and not the subjectivism that one finds in the evolutionary sciences where the researcher is trying to

---

26. Hapgood originally self-published his Acámbaro findings, and as such, that original publication is no longer available. Unfortunately, Hapgood's work is now being published by David Hatcher Childress who has been associated with the movement academics have labeled as pseudoarcheology. While that designation may indeed have some merit, Childress's introduction to Hapgood's Acámbaro work yet proves that his knowledge, is at least in some respects, superior to that of his critics. In that introduction Childress so correctly wrote: "since fossils cannot be dated by any known technical method, their age is guessed at from the geological strata around them, and since the current data of geological strata is based on the prevailing Uniformitarian theory of slow geological change, the date of many fossils may be radically closer to our own than 65 million years." (*Mystery*. 34).

27. Hapgood, *Mystery*, 82.

28. Hapgood, *Mystery*, 85.

reconstruct history. For example, if a contemporary graduate student wanted to challenge the scientific facts of the well-established gas law, PV=nRT, the law which every beginning student of chemistry and physics is familiar with, one would only need to take their challenge into a laboratory to prove their claim. However, outside of supernatural intervention, we know that that challenger's efforts would most certainly prove faulty because of the authority of that long-standing scientific law. This same scenario applies to my own scientific discoveries, which the research leading to my doctoral degree yielded. In the course of my graduate work, I synthesized novel graft copolymers never before known to humanity, i.e., macromolecules which were unique in the history of macromolecular science. Any scientist who would challenge the results of my claim to the synthesis of these new and novel graft copolymers would be readily proven wrong in the laboratory. Unfortunately, Hapgood's claim that Antarctica was recently free of its current ice cap cannot be subjected to that same type of proof. Therefore, those who control the academic journals, most probably Secular Humanists of Enlightenment ideology, will try to justify their disregard for the evidence which lends credence to Hapgood's claims which go against the faulty conclusions that Antarctica has been under a continuous thick ice-cap for millions of years.

It is here proper to emphasize that the battle for truth in the life sciences is not between scientists who control the scientific journals and scientists who know that evolutionary science is saturated with wrong conclusions. The battle for all truth, including the scientific truth revolving around the origins of the universe and the life therein, is between that evil one known as Satan and the God of Scripture who have been enemies since before the beginning of time. As the Apostle Paul wrote nearly 2000 years ago to the Christians in Ephesus, "For our struggle is not against flesh and blood, but against the rulers, against the powers, against the world forces of this darkness, against the spiritual forces of wickedness in the heavenly places."[29] Furthermore, as Jesus told the Jewish leaders who eventually were successful at having him executed for proclaiming truth about himself, "You are of your father the devil, and you want to do the desires of your father. He was a murderer from the beginning, and does not stand in the truth because there is no truth in him. Whenever he speaks a lie, he speaks from his own nature, for he is a liar and the father of lies."[30] Satan perpetuates

29. Eph 6:12.
30. John 8:44.

the lies of evolution to allow for a supposed rational, natural accounting for all living things. In so doing, people are falsely led either to believe that there is no God, or to believe in a god that is not real. Both beliefs lead to eternal condemnation. Satan has successfully convinced most Postmodern scientists that all that exists is the cosmos, as Carl Sagan so dogmatically, but so wrongly, proclaimed.

And Satan certainly had a hand in the direction that Hapgood took in the later years of his life. Mr. Hapgood must have begun to believe that there was a possibility that there exists a spiritual reality outside of the cosmos. He began to realize that the academic geologists and archeologists were purposefully obscuring the truth to uphold the dating errors of ice age timelines, to not interfere with the Darwinian theories which has dominated academic biology for more than the last century. And while Hapgood was correct to believe in the reality of the spirit world, the aspect of the spirit world that he came to know was the one that Christians seek to avoid at all cost. The great deceiver, Satan, controls that spirit world, and it is indeed a real world. Hapgood became involved in occult activity and published, with Elwood Babbit, a noted occultist, some of the dubious work involving that activity. Obviously, that involvement has not helped the cause for legitimizing his discovery of an ice-free Antarctica. Hapgood's upbringing was free of a biblical education, and he therefore would not likely have had the understanding to associate his findings of a major permanent climate change to the worldwide catastrophic flood of Noah. As I pointed out earlier, Hapgood certainly became aware that the uniformitarianism of Lyell was most probably a false conclusion, but unfortunately, he clung to his faulty theory of a shifting crust and/or pole shifts, to account for the fact of Antarctica's ice-free history. Of course, that was a major error on his part, and geologists rightfully rejected that theory, but unfortunately the fact of the ice-free Antarctica was also destroyed in the shuffle.

Those who claim that Christian faith exists without sufficient evidence, are being fatally deceived by the enemy of their souls. As the apostle wrote: "And even if our gospel is veiled, it is veiled to those who are perishing, in whose case the god of this world has blinded the minds of the unbelieving so that they might not see the light of the gospel of the glory of Christ, who is the image of God."[31]

31. 2 Cor 4: 3–4.

8

Why Existentialism Matters for the Christian

IN THIS CONCLUDING CHAPTER I emphasize why the awareness of humanistic Existentialism is of utmost importance for the Christian. As existentialistic trends in Western civilization continue to penetrate the culture of the contemporary Christian church, which acknowledges the absolute authority of Scripture, there is every reason one should expect to see negative consequences in this same church, in the same way that occurred when Enlightenment Humanism began to dominate in Western culture. Certainly, the Christian whose life is embedded in the principles of Scripture should be aware of the unfortunate consequences that Enlightenment Humanism had, and continues to have, on Christianity. I wrote about some of those negative consequences in my prior book. And of course, Christianity is still under attack by the Enlightenment Humanism stemming from the Modern era. An outstanding example of the power of the residual influence of Enlightenment Humanism is seen in the life and work of the contemporary Dr. Bart Ehrman, a Professor of Religious Studies at the University of North Carolina at Chapel Hill. Although Professor Ehrman is a graduate of Moody Bible Institute and holds his undergraduate degree from Wheaton College, he is an outspoken atheistic denier of the Christian faith, and the basis of his denial is centered in the so-called scholarship which is rooted in the rational methods of Enlightenment humanistic philosophy.

But despite the continued influence of materialistic atheism, which came to maturity with the Secular Humanism of the Modern era, Enlightenment Humanism has failed to become the dominant Humanism in

Western culture, despite the academic power behind its origin and its continued dominance in most all the academic disciplines. And even in some of the scientific disciplines, as I pointed out in an earlier chapter, the operating philosophy is often one of Postmodern Existentialism, even though when this is the case, it works under the guise of science. Therefore, the scientific mindset is today giving way to an existentialistic mindset, where—because of no perceived absolutes, i.e., no authoritative source for knowing what is real—the individual becomes interested only in whatever immediate phenomenological reality presents. Postmodern humanistic philosophy therefore results in a situation where every person is solely responsible for creating his or her own personal sense of meaning and purpose, outside of any established standards of absolute knowledge.

Unfortunately, this spirit of Existentialism is finding its way into churches which overcame the negative influence of Enlightenment Humanism. Many of these churches are now filled with those who call themselves Christian but seek their own sense of meaning and purpose through church attendance and church identification without a genuine surrender of their hearts and minds to the Lord Jesus Christ, the only means to eternal life. How many people in most contemporary Western Christian churches would be willing to obey the command that Jesus gave to the rich young ruler when he came to Jesus and asked him what he must do to inherit eternal life? Jesus reply to his question was simply another way of saying to that young man that there is no eternal life outside of the complete surrender of one's self to himself.[1] Jesus plainly taught that those who wish to retain sovereignty over their own selves will lose their selves, but those who lose their selves, for the sake of the gospel, will gain everlasting life.[2] It is the desire to promote one's self over all else that is a primary characteristic of the existentialistic mindset in our Postmodern culture.

It is interesting to consider Postmodern responses to questions asked of people regarding life's meaning and purpose. Questions such as: What are you most passionate about? How do you spend your leisure time? What are you most thankful for? What can't you live without? How would your friends describe you? These are the type of existential questions often found in personality tests, and these tests are sometimes used by organizations that focus on making romantic matches. In perusing the answers to these types of questions, I have found that most responses, coming both from

1. Mark 10: 17–22.
2. Matt 10:39.

those who call themselves "spiritual but not religious," and even many individuals who call themselves Christian, very rarely show any significant differences. In other words, when addressing these questions, there is often no reference to anything related to the metaphysical, coming from many of those who claim Christian belief. A metaphysical aspect to the meaning and purpose of life simply does not seem to be a part of the existential experience of most Postmodern people in Western culture. While this might be the expected result for those who identify with a Secular humanistic philosophy, should not a response from anyone who identifies as a Christian who is asked the question, "What are you most passionate about?" include some type of reference to the Lord Jesus Christ? This lack of commitment is all too common in the contemporary Postmodern Christian church.

The Emergent Church

While much has been written about the so-called "Emerging" church, there seems to be little acknowledgment that this movement has its roots in the onset of the Postmodern Existentialism which we are here considering. However, it is fair to say that the indicators outlined in chapter 1 of this work, where I identified three factors which show the influence of Existentialism, are certainly present in this Postmodern Christian movement. Since an entire book could be written on the subject, its thorough treatment is beyond the scope of this work, and therefore, I will be brief in the consideration of the subject. Nonetheless, the Christian should certainly be made aware of another indicator that marks the threat of Existentialism to churches which desire to remain true to God's word.

While my comments in this work on the nihilistic nature of Existentialism has sought to minimize the association of these two philosophical outlooks, there is yet an obvious and undeniable association between nihilism and Existentialism. Throughout this work I have sought to minimize that association, because if nihilism is too strongly identified with Existentialism, it can make the existentialistic worldview even more difficult to acknowledge than it is now. In other words, in the presence of the pessimism which is commonly associated with nihilism, one could easily fail to see the preponderance of Existentialism in Postmodern culture, where the absence of that pessimism is often the case.

But certainly, the signs of nihilism are strongly present in the "Emergent" church. For example, when the traditional hymns of the church are refused to be used in congregational worship, certainly the spirit of nihilism is alive and well in that Christian organization. Much of the music coming out of contemporary Christian worship is theologically shallow, and even sometimes empty of any theological content. Music has always been an integral part of Christian worship and it should serve to draw the Christian closer to God as he or she prepares their hearts to hear the proclamation and exposition of God's Word. But, for example, when the words, and even the notes, of *The Old Rugged Cross* induce embarrassment, shame, and resentment to such an extent that it, and the hundreds of works like it, are purposefully excluded in Christian worship, then there is a spirit working that is opposed to the spirit of Christ. When one refuses to enter into the spirit of Christians from earlier generations, then that nihilism will eventually be transferred from worship in general to the proclamation of God's Word, and this is indeed the progression that is being observed in many of the "Emergent" Christian churches of Western culture.

Learning from Solomon

The Christian should recognize that the existentialistic Postmodern worldview is one that is simply reappearing in the cycle of human thinking which has been working since the beginning of time. The well-known saying that "history always repeats itself" is most certainly one that bears witness to this truth. And of course, the fact that history repeats itself is because the essence of human nature is the same as it has always been. The existential worldview is clearly reflected in the Hebrew poetry of Ecclesiastes, written by King Solomon in the millennium before the appearance of Jesus of Nazareth. Solomon authored the poem near the end of his life as he reflected over a life that had been lived in constant struggle between a humanistic desire to please himself and his desire to please God. Certainly, if the great King Solomon was nearly destroyed by an existentialistic lifestyle, no Christian should think that they are not vulnerable to the same temptations that nearly destroyed Solomon.

In the second part of my earlier book, I emphasized that the primary goals of Western Modern Humanism were knowledge, social acceptance, wealth, and pleasure, in the pursuit of the emotional contentment for which all human beings naturally strive. It is the failure of those realized pursuits to satisfy that longing for emotional contentment, which produces the conditions that make ripe the appearance of existentialistic Humanism.

In contemporary Western culture the accomplishment of those goals is becoming increasingly realized by an ever-increasing proportion of the population, and as those goals are reached, it is becoming ever more apparent that the fulfillment of those goals does not lead to the expected emotional satisfaction that the human spirit desires. Satan never delivers on his promises because he is the most sophisticated liar reality has ever known. Hence existentialistic Humanism is becoming increasingly prevalent in Western culture. The reader should note that this same progression is apparent in the poetry of Solomon. From the second chapter of Ecclesiastes:

> I said to myself, "Come now, I will test you with pleasure. So enjoy yourself." And behold, it too was futility. I said of laughter, "It is madness," and of pleasure, "What does it accomplish?" I explored with my mind how to stimulate my body with wine while my mind was guiding me wisely, and how to take hold of folly, until I could see what good there is for the sons of men to do under heaven the few years of their lives. I enlarged my works: I built houses for myself, I planted vineyards for myself; I made gardens and parks for myself and I planted in them all kinds of fruit trees; I made ponds of water for myself from which to irrigate a forest of growing trees. I bought male and female slaves and I had homeborn slaves. Also I possessed flocks and herds larger than all who preceded me in Jerusalem. Also, I collected for myself silver and gold and the treasure of kings and provinces. I provided for myself male and female singers and the pleasures of men—many concubines.[3]

Solomon indeed pursued an emotional contentment by accumulating knowledge, extravagant wealth, and an abundance of women. As mentioned in the passage above, he had a harem of wives and concubines that would have made Hugh Hefner green with envy. Solomon must have had a sexual appetite for women that was second-to-none. We know that he had over 1000 women at his disposal, and that they were instrumental in turning his heart from the one true God. Solomon acknowledged the way in which he had once regarded wealth. He reflected on a humanistic understanding of life when he stated, "Men prepare a meal for enjoyment, and wine makes life merry, and money is the answer to everything."[4] Solomon was not promoting a humanistic lifestyle but was simply telling of its reality. He knew of its reality because he had been tempted to that lifestyle, and he had, at least to a certain extent, succumbed to that temptation. This example from

3. Eccl 2:1–8.
4. Eccl 10:19.

Solomon's life can help us in our focus on the issues of Humanism which I have been trying to get across to my reader. Satan begins his temptation to the humanistic mindset by his appeal to the power of human reason, and promises emotional satisfaction through the achievement of knowledge, wealth, fame, and pleasure. Solomon was blessed with an abundance of knowledge and wisdom. Furthermore, in his day, he was one of the richest persons in the world, and he had the power and fame that often comes with the achievement of great wealth.

One can think of this Humanism as representing the first stage of Satan's appeal to a humanistic philosophy, and we see parallels of this first-stage Humanism in the Enlightenment based Humanism of Western culture. This elementary Humanism is yet operational today because there are those who still seek their primary emotional contentment through the pursuit of knowledge, wealth, and pleasure. These believe that they can create their own virtue through the power of human reason, and this is the type of Humanism that yet drives contemporary philosophers such as A. C. Grayling. Grayling wants his readers to believe that they can reach ultimate emotional satisfaction through the creation of their own morality in the power of human reason.[5] But, as is observed in the life of Solomon, when these very goals of Humanism are achieved, one finds that Satan has deceived them. The humanist will always find that these common pursuits of happiness do not bring the peace and contentment which they are seeking. The fact that existentialistic philosophy is so conspicuous in Solomon's writing is evidence for the fact that existential Humanism is the Humanism to which all Humanism naturally aspires. Existentialism is a mature Humanism, and thus it should be no surprise that it has appeared in Western culture after the Humanism brought about by Enlightenment thinking. Solomon writes: "I have seen all the works which have been done under the sun, and behold, all is vanity and striving after wind. What is crooked cannot be straightened and what is lacking cannot be counted."[6] Apart from the perceived lack of purpose and meaning in human existence characterized by the declaration of that "all is vanity," we witness the characteristic existentialistic declaration of the futility of knowledge. In the first chapter, the voice of the preacher declares: "Behold, I have magnified and increased wisdom more than all who were over Jerusalem before me; and my mind has observed a wealth of wisdom and knowledge." And I set my mind to

5. Grayling, *The God Debate*, 139–75.

6. Eccl 1:14–15.

know wisdom and to know madness and folly; I realized that this also is striving after wind. Because in much wisdom there is much grief, and increasing knowledge results in increasing pain.[7]

However, despite the influence of the Humanism that nearly destroyed the great wise king Solomon, it did not have the final victory over the God centered worldview which he had held to at the beginning of his reign. Solomon began his reign with a desire to do God's will. But the human will to do God's will is always met with great opposition from that evil-deceiver who has been God's enemy from before the beginning of time. The apostle Peter reminded us that Satan attempts to destroy one's relationship with the one true God of Hebrew Scripture. The apostle wrote: "Be of sober spirit, be on the alert. Your adversary, the devil, prowls around like a roaring lion, seeking someone to devour."[8] The enemy promises satisfaction from the pursuit of fame, wealth, and pleasure. The one who has as his primary purpose in life a goal that focuses on these pursuits will always shun a proper relationship with God, and thus, that lifestyle will always result in disappointment. Solomon ultimately acknowledged that "He who loves money will not be satisfied with money, nor he who loves abundances with its income. This too is vanity."[9] The one who pursues fame, wealth, and pleasure as his primary means of emotional contentment will, in the end, come to the same conclusion that is echoed throughout Ecclesiastes. It is all vanity, and thus, Solomon's Ecclesiastes serves to declare the ultimate error of succumbing to a humanistic worldview.

But, as Augustine wrote in the beginning lines of his *Confessions*: "Thou made us for Thyself, and our hearts are restless until they rest in Thee." Solomon too eventually came to realize the truth of that oft quoted maxim of Augustine. Despite the success that Satan had in the spiritual regression of Solomon, in the end, Solomon came to his senses and concluded that all was not vanity. Solomon ends his writing with the acknowledgment of the error of his humanistic worldview. At the very end, Solomon stated: "In conclusion, when all has been heard, is: fear God and keep His commandments, because this applies to every person. For God will bring every act to judgment, everything which is hidden, whether it is good or evil."[10]

7. Eccl 1:16–18.

8. 1 Pet 5:8.

9. Eccl 5:10.

10. Eccl 12:13–14.

The Difficulty of Recognizing the Reality
of the Existentialistic Postmodern Worldview

While the dividing line between an atheistic and theistic based epistemology is distinct and objective, the dividing line between Enlightenment Humanism and the Humanism of Existentialism is exceedingly less objective, and it is this subjectivism that makes Postmodernism Existentialism often difficult to recognize and, therefore, acknowledged as a distinctive Humanism in the marketplace of philosophical ideas. This recognition becomes even more complex when one realizes that atheism and theism exist as subsets within both humanistic designations.

Those who identify with Enlightenment Humanism desire to base their epistemology in science, with pure reason as its bedrock, and thus science, for them, will always be the ultimate arbiter for forming a worldview which is based in their perceptions of reality. Existentialistic Humanism, on the other hand, will sacrifice the authority of reason for the sake of justifying any worldview that it considers convenient to self-will. Postmodern science is therefore losing authority for the average person because science has ventured into philosophical disciplines that are outside its ability to prove its philosophical contentions. Science can only affirm its contentions when the experimental methods of the laboratory can repeatably demonstrate its truth claims. Philosophical conclusions involving any aspect of metaphysical reality, even the denial of a metaphysical reality, simply cannot be based in scientific authority, and thus science has nothing to say about anything outside of the cosmos. Because of this reality, Enlightenment derived Humanism has migrated into a worldview which is almost entirely atheistic.

It is these conditions which create a quandary for the Enlightenment humanist. The Enlightenment humanist must meet the rigorous demand of reason while at the same time uphold a worldview which has been shown, repeatedly, to be irrational. It is these conflicting demands that force the Enlightenment humanist into an unwanted position of Existentialism. The difficult reality for the humanist to come to grips with is the fact that despite the many miracles that one meets in Scripture, reason will always be on the side of the God of the universe, which is exclusively the Christian God. Jesus's declaration that he was the way, the truth, and the life, cannot be broken.

So, to analyze why recognizing the existentialistic Postmodern Humanism, which is so prevalent in contemporary Western culture, is often difficult, I want to focus on two separate distinct debates which occurred between two different Christian scholars and two different atheists. Both debates revolved around the atheist's claim that belief in God is delusionary. The first debate for consideration occurred in 2007 between the renowned Oxford Professor Richard Dawkins, and his fellow Oxford colleague and mathematician Dr. John Lennox, who is also known for his unwavering Christian faith. The Fixed Point Foundation sponsored the event for the purpose of addressing some of the issues which were published in Dawkins's then new book, *The God Delusion*. The debate can be viewed online in its entirety.[11] As the debate was approaching its end, the question: "Do we need God to be moral?" was put to both sides, and it is in Dawkins's answer to this question where his Existentialism becomes clear.

The second example will focus on a debate between Professor William Lane Craig and Professor Mike Begon, an ecologist at the University of Liverpool, which took place in Liverpool, also in 2007. The reader can also view this debate online it its entirety.[12] In the discipline of Christian apologetics, Dr. Craig is well known for his debates with those who hold to atheistic worldviews. Craig is the best theistic debater who has ever taken to the debate stage; his gift for the art is amazing. He is willing to debate the question of God's existence with anyone, no matter how impressive are their credentials, and he always gives a rationally defensive position. In the introduction to this work, I noted that Dr. Craig, on a Christian radio talk show, made the declaration that Postmodernism was a myth, "perpetrated in our churches by misguided youth pastors." I think perhaps because of his denial of the reality of the Postmodern worldview Craig does not understand that many of those with whom he engages in debate, despite coming from a scientific position, are coming from an existentialistic Postmodern philosophy. This debate between Craig and Begon serves particularly well to bring the truth of this claim to light.

The Lennox/Dawkins Debate

In this debate, when the issue of the question of whether or not morality was possible without God, Dawkins appealed to the universality of the human conscience, by referring to it as "something in the air," to suggest a universal idea of right vs. wrong. The point that Dawkins was unconsciously

11. Dawkins vs Lennox, "The God Delusion Debate." Fixed Point Foundation. 2007.

12. Craig vs Begon, "Public Debate: Is God a Delusion?" Reasonable Faith Tour, 2007.

making, was that because of the human conscience, God is not necessary for a standard of morality. While Lennox, incorrectly conceded, for the sake of charity, that an atheist can be good,[13] he correctly pointed out that that universal idea of morality (i.e., the human conscience, although neither debater referred to it as that) was evidence for the fact that the biblical claim, that we are moral beings made in the image of God, is true. In his answer, Lennox did an excellent job of showing that Dawkins's atheistic philosophy supplied no basis for even discussing the issue of morality because of his philosophy, which even by Dawkins's own admission, denies even the existence of good and evil. Lennox showed that Dawkins's admission to the function of human conscience, to serve as evidence for the existence of morality, was contrary to Dawkins's prior writings where he held to the Darwinian idea of survival of the fittest. However, despite what Dawkins believes, human beings have a place in the universe which is unique to all other life, evidence of which is the very conscience that Dawkins has indirectly alluded to. When my pet cat comes trotting into my yard with a severely injured baby rabbit between its jaws there is no violation of any moral law. But when my neighbor decides to kill her unborn baby, because raising that child would present to her an inconvenience, the natural human conscience, of which even Dawkins acknowledges exists, should indeed be affected. If the conscience is not disturbed under such circumstances, then that conscience must be described as one that is seared or broken.[14]

---

13. Admittedly, this is a subtle but critical criticism of Lennox on this point. I think that Lennox should have stated instead, that an atheist can sometimes behave in such a way as to give an *appearance* of righteousness. However, just because a particular human behavior or action is congruous with the laws of the Hebrew God, does not mean that that action is coming from a moral criterion. Unless the action is done from a conscious will to do the will of God, the action cannot be considered truly moral in the purest sense. And this is the reason that Scripture continually drives home the point that no one, outside of the imputed righteousness of Christ, can will the moral good. As the apostle declared, "there is none that is righteous, (i.e., truly moral) no, not one." (Rom 3:10). I pointed out in my prior book the ultimate criterium for any concept of morality is the will of God, as it has been revealed in Scripture. Hitler was kind and generous to his German Shepherd dogs, which certainly may have appeared, to an outside observer, as moral behavior, but I think that we all can agree that Hitler was anything but a moral person. Therefore, I think that Lennox did a disservice to Dawkins, by perhaps giving him the impression that he is capable of morality within the power of his own human nature. That is a serious fallacy, because unless Dawkins comes to his senses, he will eventually be judged as evil by the ultimate judge, (whom we all will soon face) unless he repents and acknowledges Jesus Christ as his savior.

14. 1 Tim 4:2.

The point that I am making is that Dawkins's Darwinism forces him into an Existentialistic Humanism (even though he tries to keep his Enlightenment rationality) by being forced to acknowledge a morality that naturally exists in the human conscience. Dawkins would be more honest with himself, and with those he influences, if he would call himself an existentialistic philosopher with an interest in the theory of Darwinian evolution. If he did that, he could go back to his prior philosophy, and stand with Sartre, who boldly proclaimed that without God anything is permissible.

Before leaving this point for the next one, we should briefly note how Dawkins rationalized his subtle admission of a natural standard for morality (which is his acknowledgment of the human conscience) to try to keep it compatible with his Darwinism. Dawkins was careful to insist that this idea of a communal determination of right vs. wrong did not remain constant with time. In other words what might be considered right in the current contemporary setting could have been quite different 200 years ago. In making this declaration he was simply trying to take away the concept of an absolute morality with his admission of this phenomenon, which in turn would minimize its clash with his Darwinism. And it must be conceded that Dawkins is correct in claiming that this naturally recognized sense of right and wrong (again this is the conscience—although he does not call it that) is not an absolute standard for morality. But what Dawkins does not understand is that when the conscience is working properly, i.e., when the conscience is not seared, it will always condemn what the God-given moral law condemns. Before the atheistic Freud came on the scene, adultery was widely acknowledged as morally wrong, even in secular society and, as I mentioned in my earlier book, even both Plato and Aristotle acknowledged adultery as morally wrong, simply based on a properly working conscience. The fact that adultery is now often overlooked as moral deficiency is only proof of the moral decline currently being witnessed on a grand scale in Western culture, brought on by the Humanism of which Dawkins so powerfully and proudly promotes.

As the debate was nearing its end, Lennox made the comment that the risen Christ had conquered death, at which point Dawkins said sarcastically, "And so it comes down to the resurrection of Jesus, does it?" That question shows particularly well the irrationality of Dawkins mind. Well of course Dr. Dawkins, one can validly declare that it does indeed come down to that fact. If the crucified Jesus of Nazareth was in fact resurrected, then any non-Christian system of epistemology, including your own, is absolutely annihilated. The ultimate question that anyone should thus ask himself is, Was Jesus, in fact, destroyed?" Were the Jewish and Roman authorities successful in their attempts to kill him, and keep him in the tomb? The answer to this question, supplies the basis for the belief which confirms or destroys every other belief of the search for ultimate truth. The evidence of Scripture clearly supports a physical risen Christ, if for no other reason, simply by the fact that he appeared to so many people after his resurrection who all bore witness to seeing him in person.[15]

The Craig/Begon Debate

The same essential issues described in the earlier debate are present in this debate between Craig and Begon. Dr. Begon began by asserting that belief in God's existence is delusional, and then he claimed that he does not assert that God does not exist. Begon cannot directly say that God does not exist, to maintain consistency with his claim to scientific rationality, because he realizes that there is no way to prove a claim that there is no God. But nonetheless, his position, as Dr. Craig pointed out, is one of irrationality unless he changes the meaning of the word delusional to mean something that it does not mean. The fact that Begon's arguments were pointed out to be irrational simply did not seem to matter to Begon. Begon's contention is that any belief is delusional when there is insufficient evidence to believe in it. Of course, Craig correctly pointed out that there are beliefs that can be correctly held without the evidence of proof. One can believe, on a sun-filled day, that somewhere in the world it is pouring down rain, having no proof of the fact and yet that certainly would not be considered a delusional belief.

But at the debate's end Begon's philosophy was particularly well exposed for what it really is. Begon is simply a good example of an existentialist who is working under the guise of science. When questions from the audience were entertained, Begon was approached by a psychiatric nurse who shared his experiences with working with delusional patients. The nurse pointed out that a psychiatric patient who suffers from delusional thoughts is characterized by holding to a "fixed, false belief that is neither open to reason or experience." And then the questioner made the point that atheists attribute "chance" as the overriding mechanism for the operation of all reality and then pointed out that that model was inconsistent with what was observed in reality. Begon responded by saying that he would not be forced into a position which held that "chance" was responsible for the

15. 1 Cor 5:5–6.

existence of the universe. Begon continued, "It would be equally deluded to believe in chance, a name given to something I don't understand, as to believe in God, a name given to something I don't understand." And then Begon made the declaration that shows particularly well his Existentialism. As if to say he could really care less for understanding the origin of the universe, he stated, "I take a much more practical view. I deal in the here and now. I deal in what's going to happen tomorrow. I deal in trying to do good today, as good as I can." That Craig does not see the dominance of an existentialistic worldview reflected in Begon's arguments is indeed surprising.

The Christian Must be Aware of the Philosophical Bias in Postmodern Science

Therefore, in both examples presented above, a philosophy of Existentialism was obviously working, even though both debates should have been controlled by an epistemology that is consistent with pure logic. In other words, in Postmodern science, violation of the laws of logic is happening because of the Existentialism that is having increasing influence in Postmodern Humanism. The primary driving force for this violation of logic is an overwhelming desire to exclude the truth of the deity of Jesus of Nazareth from the Western educational system, even though the logic of science does not force that exclusion. Since, in Western culture, science is viewed as the ultimate authority for the basis of all knowledge, there is a strong impetus in science to drive the timeline of the creation event as far back in history as is conceivable, to make it more workable for the acceptance of an atheistic Darwinian evolutionary worldview.

I think it noteworthy that science is showing compatibility with the biblical account of creation. We know from Scripture that the universe is not eternal, i.e., that it had a beginning, and science has confirmed this truth of Scripture. Science is now showing compatibility with the first three recorded words of Scripture, "In the beginning." It is this scientific reality that Dr. Craig is fond of using in his Kalem cosmological argument for proving the existence of God. But if science still refuses to acknowledge the truth of the universal flood of Noah, then this puts all scientific method on date-setting into question, because the reality of that catastrophic event proves that the structure of physical reality was changed in ways that science has not even begun to contemplate. As was presented in the last chapter, there is convincing evidence that science has the extinction date of the dinosaurs wrong, and this evidence is deliberately ignored. The teaching that dinosaurs became extinct because of asteroid strikes, millions of years ago, is far from being evidence based. It is simply willful speculation to prevent science from acknowledging that the dinosaurs were most likely made extinct by the universal worldwide flood of Noah.

Notwithstanding the appreciation for, and admiration of, Professor Craig's debating skills, I must admit that I am troubled by his acceptance, at face value, of some of the scientific claims that are made by humanistic scientists in the discipline of cosmology. I am a trained scientist in the study of physical reality at the molecular level, and I readily acknowledge that my understanding of astrophysics and cosmology is limited. Nonetheless, I am skeptical of the accuracy of some of the claims that are being stated as fact in the disciplines of cosmology and astrophysics, namely the claim that the universe came into existence around 13–15 billion years ago, a figure that Professor Craig seems to readily accept.

That dating is based on Hubble's red shift data, which he generated as an observational astronomer at the Mount Wilson observatory in the 20s and 30s. As I presented in the last chapter with the review of some of Hapgood's work, reconstruction of past events can be subject to error, and certainly when one speaks of the events which describe the beginning of creation, much speculation is involved, particularly since models which are based on currently observed phenomenon do not necessarily extrapolate linearly, backwards to t=0. Because space and time are certainly interrelated, and the fact that both entities were coming into existence at the creation event, the accuracy of a date placed upon that event should always be questioned, for the simple reason that no one, apart from the creator, was there to see it, and therefore no one really knows for certain the physics at $t = 5.0 \times 10^{-10}$ seconds. Science must be based on observation, but science has no way to observe that specific point in time. Therefore, one cannot claim with certainty that the creation event occurred 14 billion years ago. As I noted in the last chapter, Hapgood realized that the geological timelines which assume Lyell's principle of Uniformitarianism are subject to error, and the false assumptions of Uniformitarianism are the primary reason that humanistic scientists cannot acknowledge the fact of the universal worldwide flood, which was an actual event, which occurred somewhere within a timespan of a few thousand years ago. If both Modern and Postmodern science cannot even acknowledge the worldwide flood of Noah, let alone try to date that event, which is much less technically involved than is dating the beginning of the universe, what should make anyone think that it has the date of the creation event correct? If Professor Craig wants to immerse himself in the methods of science, he would better spend his significant talent in defending the fact of the worldwide flood. There is simply an undeniable philosophical bias in science against any worldview which aligns with the truth of Scripture. It is necessary for the Christian to know that the residual Enlightenment humanism, which theoretically should be based in the authority of reason, of necessity, must break down, and this is what is happening with the rise of the Postmodern Humanism of Existentialism.

Summing it Up

In my writing on Western Humanism, I have sought to make my reader aware that the Christian influence in Western culture continues its decline through the influence of the philosophy of Existentialism. It is exceedingly important for any person to come to the realization that there is only one path, of two alternative paths, which one can travel that leads to eternal life. Jesus very carefully delineated those two paths with such clarity that any mind should be able to understand the reality of the choice that lies before all who have the capacity to choose. Jesus specifically told his listeners that there was a wide path of travel which is opposed to the narrow path leading to everlasting life. Jesus made it known that the wide road, which most people choose to follow, is a path that leads to everlasting destruction, and Jesus could have very well labeled that road as "Humanism Road." Indeed, that road is increasingly becoming a crowded road, and the social pressure in contemporary Postmodern Western culture to walk it is increasingly unrelenting. Any observant participant in Western culture should be able to understand that the social pressure to walk that wide road is coming at us from every angle, including the institutions of government, education, commerce, religion, and particularly the mass media. It is my sincere hope and prayer that my writing on Western Humanism has enabled the reader to understand the importance of having the courage to leave that broad road of Humanism and walk the narrow road with Jesus, the Christ, which few people have been predestined to walk.[16]

16. Matt 7:13, Eph 1:11.

Appendix

IN CHAPTER 7 I discussed how even a child gains an understanding of what is real, which is related to the subject of epistemology in philosophy. There, I used a simple illustration of a toddler sitting in toy-like toddler-chairs—one designed to support the toddler's weight and another designed to deceive—to show how we as human beings use subconscious rational processing, involving presupposition, for gaining an understanding of a true representation of reality. There is nothing more important in anyone's life than gaining an understanding of the existential reality that is based in truth. Such an understanding will always include the knowledge that the enemy of every person's soul is that great deceiver Satan, who is so well revealed in Holy Scripture. The illustration of sitting in a chair is a simple, but powerful, demonstration of how the intellectual concept of trust becomes crucial to gaining a proper understanding of reality. When reviewing that thought, I recalled an earlier writing where I used the illustration of "chair-sitting" to reduce the essential theological truth of Scripture to as few words as possible.

Many years ago, a few weeks after receiving my undergraduate degree, I felt compelled to write a simple gospel tract in order to share my Christian faith, and because of its relevance to the topic of this discussion in particular, I here reproduce that entire tract in this appendix. It reads as follows:[1]

The Gospel Truth About Your Existence

> The problems of the human race are obvious. We hate, lie, cheat, steal, rob, murder, fight and lust for that which we do not have.

1. All Scripture is from KJV.

137

Furthermore, these problems are universal, as any newspaper of any culture or civilization will confirm. Did you ever notice how easy it was to stretch the truth when you found yourself in a "fix"? You did it naturally, did you not? In other words, the problem of lying is within our nature. It is natural for us to seek our own. The Bible speaks much of our self-seeking nature. In Philippians 2:21 we read, "for all seek their own . . . ." In Isaiah 53: 6, "All we like sheep have gone astray; we have turned everyone to his own way." The Bible calls this problem sin, and it states that we are all guilty. Romans 3:23 states, "For all have sinned and come short of the glory of God." Again, in Psalms 14:3 we read, "They are all gone aside, they are all together become filthy: There is none that doeth good, no not one."

How can we, as described above, be united to a perfect, holy and loving God, the ultimate Good? Friend, we cannot. For the consequences of this sinful nature is death. Declares Romans 5:12, "Wherefore, as by one man (Adam) sin entered into the world, and death by sin: and so death passed upon all men, for that all have sinned." James 1:15 tells us, ". . . sin when it is finished bringeth forth death." By death the Bible is not referring to mere physical death. II Thessalonians 1:9 makes plain that the sinner "shall be punished with everlasting destruction."

If this message ended here it would be one of doom. But it does not, because God has provided for us a way back to Himself. John 3:16 reads "For God so loved the world, that He gave His only begotten Son, that whosoever believeth in Him should not perish, but have everlasting life." God gave of Himself, the Lord Jesus Christ, to take the penalty of death that we as sinners deserved. "But God commendeth His love toward us in that while we were yet sinners, Christ died for us" (Romans 5:8). By believing on Christ one can escape eternal destruction.

What does it mean to believe in Jesus? To illustrate, we can use the example of a chair. Believing in a chair is putting your faith in the fact that it will do what it claims to do. It claims to support you. You do not put your faith in the chair simply by saying that you think it will hold you; but your faith becomes real when you sit on it. You appropriate the chair. Believing on Jesus by faith is the same. You put your faith in Jesus by believing that He will do what He claims He will do. Jesus claims to be able to reconcile you with God and save you from eternal destruction. He said in John 14:6, "I am the way, the truth and the life, no one cometh unto the Father but by Me." You do not put your faith in Jesus by simply saying that you believe in His existence. Your faith in Christ becomes saving faith when you appropriate Christ's sacrifice by yielding your heart, that is, your very most inner being, to Him. "For by grace are ye saved through faith, not of works lest any man should boast" (Ephesians 2:8,9).

Friend, whatever your circumstances, you can now, from a sincere heart pray this prayer: "God be merciful to me a sinner" (Luke 18:13). In Romans 10:13 we read, "For whosoever shall call upon the name of the Lord shall be saved." By your faith in Christ, God now declares you righteous.

If you have made the decision to follow Christ by faith, your life will never be the same. God's Spirit will abide within you and give you a new nature. Jesus refers to this in John 3:7 as being "born again." In II Corinthians 5:17 we read, "Therefore if any man be in Christ, he is a new creature: old things are passed away; behold, all things are become new."

All of man's problems, including yours, are due to his selfish sinful nature. Because of God's perfect nature we are therefore separated from Him, unless we accept God's provision to come back to Him.

If you have accepted Christ, you will want to grow spiritually by attending a church that teaches and preaches the Bible.

Bibliography

Afetinan, A. *Life and Works of Piri Re'is: The Oldest Map of America*. Translated by L. Yolac and D. Uzmen. 2nd ed. Ankara, Turkey: Turkish Historical Society, 1987.

Aksan, Virginia. *The Early Modern Ottomans: Remapping the Empire*. Edited by V. H. Askan and D. Goffman. Cambridge: Cambridge University Press, 2007.

Alexander, Eben. *Proof of Heaven: A Neurosurgeon's Journey into the Afterlife*. New York: Simon & Schuster, 2012.

Barnes, Wesley. *The Philosophy and Literature of Existentialism*. Barron's Educational Series, New York: Woodbury, 1968.

Beltz, Emily. "Pastor Arrested for Protesting State Ag's Decision on Marriage Law." *World Magazine*, July 12, 2013. https://world.wng.org/2013/07/pastor_arrested_for_protesting_state_ags_decision_on_marriage_law.

Bugliosi, Vincent. *Divinity of Doubt: The God Question*. Perseus, PA: Vanguard, 2011.

Bukdahl, Jorgen. *Søren Kierkegaard & The Common Man*. Translated, revised, and edited by Bruce H. Kirmmse. Grand Rapids: Eerdmans, 2001.

Carnell, John Edward. *An Introduction to Christian Apologetics*. Grand Rapids: Eerdmans, 1948.

Carter, John D. "Re-evaluation of Orientation Effects in the Friction of a Hard Ellipsoid Sliding on Rubber." *Journal of Applied Physics* 93.2 (2003) 1283–86.

——. *Western Humanism: A Christian Perspective-Understanding Moral Decline in Western Culture*. North Canton, OH: Photon, 2005.

Cochrane, Arthur C. *The Existentialists and God*. Philadelphia: Westminster, 1956.

Craig, William Lane vs Begon, Mike. "Public Debate: Is God a Delusion?" Reasonable Faith Tour, University of Liverpool, March 7 2007. https://youtu.be/uuKZjMUoh3o.

——. vs Penner, Myron. "Should Christians Abandon Apologetics?" Up for Debate hosted by Julie Roys, Moody Radio, April 2016, https://www.youtube.com/watch?v=Iz6Z9PwNQuA.

Dawkins, Richard. *The God Delusion*. New York: Bantam, 2006.

——. *The Greatest Show on Earth: The Evidence for Evolution*. New York: Free Press, 2009.

——. vs Lennox, John. "The God Delusion Debate" Fixed Point Foundation, https://www.youtube.com/watch?v=zF5bPI92–50, Oct 3, 2007.

Findlay, J. N. *Hegel: A Re-examination*. New York: Oxford University Press, 1976.

Firger, Jessica. "Science's Reproducibility Problem: 100 Psych Studies Were Tested and Only Half Held Up." *Newsweek*, August 28, 2015. https://www.newsweek.com/reproducibility-science-psychology-studies-366744.

Fleegler, E. W., et. al. "Firearm Legislation and Firearm-Related Fatalities in the United States." *Journal of the American Medical Association* 173.9 (2013) 732–40. doi:10.1001/jamainternmed.2013.1286.

Flint, Robert. *Anti-Theistic Theories: The Baird Lecture for 1877.* Edinburgh: Blackwood, 1879.

Fudge, Edward William. *The Fire That Consumes: A Biblical and Historical Study of the Doctrine of Final Punishment.* Eugene, OR: Cascade, 2011.

Grayling, A. C. *The God Argument: The Case Against Religion and for Humanism.* London: Bloomsbury, 2013.

Hapgood, Charles H. *Earth's Shifting Crust: A Key to Some Basic Problems of Earth Science.* New York: Pantheon, 1958.

———. *Maps of the Ancient Sea Kings: Evidence of Advanced Civilization in the Ice Age.* Philadelphia: Chilton, 1966.

———. *Mystery in Acámbaro: An account of the Ceramic Collection of the Late Waldemar Julsrud, in Acámbaro, Gto. Mexico.* Kempton, IL: Adventures Unlimited, 2000.

Harris, Sam. *The End of Faith: Religion, Terror and the Future of Reason.* New York: Norton, 2004.

Hegel, Georg Wilhelm Friedrich. *The Philosophy of History.* Translated by J. Sibree. Great Books of the Western World, Encyclopedia Britannica, edited by R.M. Hutchins, 1952.

Hitchens, Christopher. *God Is Not Great: How Religion Poisons Everything.* New York: Hachette, 2007.

Hume, David. *An Enquiry Concerning Human Understanding.* Great Books of the Western World, Encyclopedia Britannica, edited by R.M. Hutchins, 1952.

Jaspers, Karl. *Existentialism and Humanism, Three Essays.* Edited by Hanns E. Fischer. Translated by E. B. Ashton. New York: Moore, 1952.

———. *Man in the Modern Age.* London: Routledge & Paul, 1951.

James, William. *Essays on Faith and Morals.* New York: Meridian, 1962.

Keach, Sean. "Eternal Life: Want to Live Forever? You Just Have to Make It to 2050, Experts Say." *The Sun,* January 17, 2020. https://www.thesun.co.uk/tech/5587710/how-to-live-forever/.

Keller, Werner. *The Bible as History.* 2nd rev. ed. Translated by William Neil and B. H. Rasmussen. New York: Barnes and Noble, 1995.

Kierkegaard, Søren. *Concluding Unscientific Postscript,* Translated by David Swenson. Princeton: Princeton University Press, 1944.

———. *The Sickness unto Death.* London: Penguin, 1989.

Lewis, C. S. *Mere Christianity.* New York: Macmillan, 1952.

———. *The Problem of Pain.* New York: Macmillan, 1962.

Luther, Martin. *Table Talks.* Edited by Thomas S. Kepler. Mineola, NY: Dover, 2005.

McDonald, William. "Søren Kierkegaard." *The Stanford Encyclopedia of Philosophy,* Winter 2017 Edition. Edited by Edward N. Zalta. https://plato.stanford.edu/search/r?entry=/entries/kierkegaard/&page=1&total_hits=78&pagesize=10&archive=win2017&rank=0&query=kierkegaard.

Morse, Melvin, with Paul Perry. *Closer to the Light: Learning from the Near-death Experiences of Children.* New York: Villard, 1990.

Morrison, David. "Man for the Cosmos: Carl Sagan's Life and Legacy as Scientist, Teacher, And Skeptic." *Skeptical Inquirer* 31.1 (2007) 29–36.

Neal, Mary C. *To Heaven and Back: A True Story.* Colorado Springs, CO: Water Brook, 2011.

Olson, Robert G. *An Introduction to Existentialism,* New York: Dover, 1962.

Bibliography

Plato. *The Dialogues of Plato, Laws VIII, (841)*. Translated by Benjamin Jowett. Great Books of the Western World, Encyclopedia Britannica, edited by R. M. Hutchins, 1952.

Ruby, Abraham P. https://www.google.com/books/edition/_/LQ5kPQAACAAJ?hl=en

Rushton, J. Philippe, and Aurther R. Jensen. "James Watson's Most Inconvenient Truth: Race Realism and the Moralistic Fallacy." *Medical Hypotheses* 71.5 (2008) 626–40.

Schaeffer, Francis A. *Escape from Reason*. Downers Grove, IL: InterVarsity, 1966.

Sartre, Jean-Paul. *Existentialism and Humanism*. Translation and Introduction by Philip Mairet. Brooklyn, NY: Haskell, 1946.

Sahakian, William S., and Mabel L. Sahakian. *Ideas of the Great Philosophers*. New York: Barnes and Noble, 1966.

Scott, Eugene. "Black Lives Matter Protesters Confront Clinton at a Fundraiser." *CNN*, February 25, 2016. http://www.cnn.com/2016/02/25/politics/hillary-clinton-black-lives-matter-whichhillary/.

Strong, Augustus Hopkins. *Great Poets and Their Theology*. Philadelphia: American Baptist Publication Society, 1897.

Thilly, Frank, and Ledger Wood. *A History of Philosophy*. New York: Holt, Rinehart and Winston, 1964.

Warburton, Nigel. "A Student's Guide to Jean-Paul Sartre's Existentialism and Humanism." *Philosophy Now* 15 (Spring/Summer 1996).

Wells, David F. *Above All Earthly Pow'rs: Christ in a Postmodern World*. Grand Rapids: Eerdmans, 2005.

Index

Index

Index

volition, 4, 9–10, 12–14, 29–33, 42, 46, 52, 54–55, 57, 60, 64, 66
Voltaire, 23, 54

Watson, James D., 37–38
wealth, 14–15, 73–74, 76, 125–28
Wells, David, xxiii, 69–70

Wikipedia, 101, 118
Wittgenstein, Ludwig, 16
worldview (definition of), xi
WWI, 53, 67, 86
WWII, 28, 53, 67, 72, 75, 86, 102

Xenophanes, xx, xxv

Made in the USA
Las Vegas, NV
19 June 2021

25031604R00098